Stundenblätter
Golding
»Lord of the Flies«

Gerd Kaiser

# Stundenblätter
# Golding
# »Lord of the Flies«

42 Seiten Beilage

Ernst Klett Verlag

Reihe: Stundenblätter Englisch

Als Textgrundlage wurde die unter der Nummer 0.571.08483.4 bei Faber and Faber Ltd. erschienene Ausgabe des Romans genommen. Alle Seitenangaben beziehen sich auf diese Ausgabe.

CIP-Kurztitelaufnahme der Deutschen Bibliothek

**Kaiser, Gerd:**
Stundenblätter Golding, „Lord of the Flies" / Gerd Kaiser.
2. Aufl. – Stuttgart: Klett, 1987.
(Reihe: Stundenblätter Englisch)
ISBN 3-12-925162-6

ISBN 3-12-925162-6

2. Auflage 1987

Satz: G. Müller, Heilbronn; Wilhelm Röck, Weinsberg
Druck: Wilhelm Röck, Weinsberg
Einbandgestaltung: Zembsch' Werkstatt, München

# Contents


**Reading an English Novel** . . . . . . . . . . 7

**Plan of the Unit "Lord of the Flies"** . . . . . . . . . . 14

**Notes on Interpretation** . . . . . . . . . . 19

**Lesson Plans** . . . . . . . . . . 74

*Chapters I to III: "We've got to have rules."* . . . . . . . . . . 74

| | | |
|---|---|---|
| Lesson 1: | Introduction of the Topic/The Initial Situation . . . . . | 74 |
| Lesson 2: | The Summons of the Conch . . . . . | 76 |
| Lesson 3: | Steps Towards Democratic Order . . . . . | 77 |
| Lesson 4: | "Democracy" at Work: The Second Meeting . . . . . | 79 |
| Lesson 5: | The Fire . . . . . | 81 |
| Lesson 6: | Three Boys and their Ways . . . . . | 82 |

*Chapters IV to VI: "Things are breaking up."* . . . . . . . . . . 83

| | | |
|---|---|---|
| Lesson 7: | Natural Belligerence versus Social Conditioning . . . . . | 83 |
| Lesson 8: | The Knife and the Glasses . . . . . | 84 |
| Lesson 9: | Rational Action versus Irrational Action: The Third Assembly . . . . . | 86 |
| Lesson 10: | The "Beast" – Product of Human Imagination . . . . . | 87 |

*Chapters VII to IX: "We're going to have fun on this island."* . . . . . . . . . . 89

| | | |
|---|---|---|
| Lessons 11/12: | "Daylight Sanity" and Anarchic Impulses . . . . . | 89 |
| Lessons 13/14: | Simon and the "Lord of the Flies" . . . . . | 91 |

*Chapters X to XII: "Never mind what's sense. That's gone."* . . . . . . . . . . 94

| | | |
|---|---|---|
| Lesson 15: | Vision and Blindness . . . . . | 94 |
| Lesson 16: | The Possibilities of Irresponsible Authority . . . . . | 96 |
| Lesson 17: | Defiance of Fatal Knowledge . . . . . | 98 |
| Lesson 18: | The Holocaust and the Rescue . . . . . | 99 |
| Lessons 19/20: | The Parable of Man's Fall . . . . . | 100 |

| | | |
|---|---|---|
| Additional Lesson: | The Theory of Innate Aggressiveness . . . . . | 104 |
| Additional Lesson: | Structural Elements in LoF . . . . . | 107 |

**Student Papers** . . . . . . . . . . . . . . . . . . . . . . . . . . . . . . . . . . . . . . . . . . . . . . . 111

*Material and/or Expected Results for Student Papers* . . . . . . . . . . . . . . . . . . . . 112

**Annotations/Vocabulary** . . . . . . . . . . . . . . . . . . . . . . . . . . . . . . . . . . . . . 126

**Selected Bibliography** . . . . . . . . . . . . . . . . . . . . . . . . . . . . . . . . . . . . . . 143

# Reading an English Novel

According to all the curricula of the Länder of the German Federal Republic, students at the "Sekundarstufe II" level are required to read and analyse English and American literary texts. They must be able to summarize texts, to paraphrase them, and to comment on them. They are to be led from a predominantly receptive attitude towards an increasingly independent, systematic, critical approach to the literary work of art. At the same time the students' occupation with literary texts is expected to develop their understanding of the world, and ultimately of themselves, of their own position in the pattern of human existence.

There is general agreement in the Länder curricula that "Sekundarstufe II" students, besides reading short stories and other relatively short English texts, should be encouraged to read longer texts, too, such as novels or plays. With regard to novels there is common consent that books must be chosen whose contents and theme would appeal to young adolescents, arouse their interest and motivate them enough to deal with the books at some length. Bearing this aspect in mind, there are not too many novels to choose from.

Once the decision has been made as to which English or American novel is to be discussed in class (and Golding's *Lord of the Flies* is in many ways a perfect choice), both teacher and students are faced with some fundamental difficulties. In most instances, the German students must learn how to read longer texts; i.e. they must be familiarized with the technique of extensive reading. As there are only a limited number of teaching hours available in which to deal with a full length book, and as the students are meant to enjoy their reading, they must be allowed to cover large parts of the novel just reading "for gist", without looking up every unknown word. In principle, they should read the book from beginning to end, as they would in German, and the discussion of the novel in class ought to concentrate on essential issues, main developments, key passages.

Novels that are clearly structured in themselves (such as D. H. Lawrence's *Sons and Lovers,* Thomas Hardy's *Tess of the d'Urbervilles,* G. Orwell's *1984,* or even J. Salinger's *Catcher in the Rye*) can be read extensively in such a way, with a subsequent division into main parts to be discussed separately and successively, with an analysis of plot and character developments, of important passages or "scenes" – possibly from certain "plateaus" that allow the tracing of the main threads in the fabric of the novel under discussion – and a final comprehensive analysis incorporating the information gathered and discussed previously.

However, not every novel lends itself to this kind of extensive reading.

A book such as Golding's *Lord of the Flies (= LoF)* is far too meticulously composed and structured to be considered as a whole from the start. In fact, knowing the end of the novel when discussing the beginning would totally spoil the effect and would grossly destroy the finely woven pattern of the step-by-step development of the novel.

For this reason, in order to guarantee an adequate methodological approach to

*LoF*, the concept of extensive reading needs a slight modification. The students are not encouraged to read the whole novel from beginning to end beforehand. Instead, they are asked to read the 12 chapters of the novel (approx. 18 pages each) in a staggered sequence of five parts that constitute meaningful units:

- first the whole of Chapter I,
- then Chapters II and III,
- after that Chapters IV–VI,
- Chapters VII–IX,
- Chapters X–XII,

as the text analysis proceeds in class.

In each of these five units the development of motifs and themes will be traced, whilst every lesson concentrates on one major thematic focus.

To guide the students in their reading for gist, every chapter of *LoF* should be subdivided, and the students should be required to provide every part with a brief headline or written summary. Additionally, some passages in every chapter should be covered intensively in close reading; the relevant pages are announced for each chapter. These passages will be discussed in class at some detail.

Thus, the students are familiarized with cursory chapter-to-chapter reading and learn to cover ground quickly, while keeping their attention on important details. This approach might be called "modified extensive reading", in so far as the tracing of the gradual development of the action as well as of the symbolism involved is considered indispensable and is not sacrificed to a necessarily more superficial summarizing of larger parts of the novel.

## William Golding's "Lord of the Flies"

*LoF* was Golding's first novel to be published (1954). It met with an enthusiastic response both in Britain and the USA (especially from adolescents) almost immediately, and ever since has fascinated readers all over the world.

None of Golding's later novels [*Pincher Martin* (1957), *Free Fall* (1959); *The Inheritors* (1962), *The Spire* (1964), *The Pyramid* (1969); *Darkness Visible* (1979)] has equalled the success of *LoF*; and when, in 1983, Golding's career as a writer was crowned with the award of the Nobel Prize for Literature, some critics voiced the opinion that this honour was bestowed on him above all because of the great success of his firstling *LoF*.

The story of British schoolboys wrecked on a South Sea island found its way into German grammar schools in the early sixties and has since then been one of the most frequently read English novels in schools.

The immediate model for Golding's *LoF* is R. M. Ballantyne's classic adventure book *The Coral Island* (1858) which Golding both parallels and parodies; we are also reminded of D. Defoe's *Robinson Crusoe* (1719), and R. L. Stevenson's *Treasure Island* (1883), A. Ransome's *Swallows and Amazons* (1930), R. Hughes' *A High Wind in Jamaica* (1929), or even R. Macaulay's *Orphan Island* (1924), which all belong to the ancestry of island adventure books without having any direct connection with Golding's novel.

In Ballantyne's *Coral Island* Ralph, Jack and Peterkin are optimistic, orderly, typically honourable British boys who see their South Sea island as a gorgeous paradise; they tackle all their problems bravely and successfully, as adults would, and they maintain their British middle-class standards throughout.

Golding's *LoF,* too, is first and foremost a book about boys who behave (and speak) like real children when their plane crashes and they are stranded on an uninhabited tropical island; they, too, start out by seeing their new experience as an exciting adventure. Typically, the older boys are reminded of the famous island books they know, after they realize they are on a coral island. (cf. p. 38)

However, while at first they manage to adjust to the island and to maintain themselves quite well (they discover how to make fire, they build shelters, organize their food problem) and even to establish some order (they have assemblies, divide up social responsibilities), the boys' outlook on their island life soon changes. Rather than think of rescue and try to use reason, common sense and their "daylight sanity", most of the boys succumb to irrational fears and irrational "games". They soon start disputes, turn against each other, become destructive, and eventually lapse into a form of primitive savagery following their innermost dark primeval impulses.

Golding's *LoF* in its relentless progression from the paradisiac beginning (though set against the background of an atomic war!) to the infernal fire that destroys the whole island in the end, is ultimately concerned with very fundamental questions concerning our "civilized" society, the veneer of Western education and culture. It deals with the essential nature of man, with societal responsibility, morality, the existence and growth of evil (as symbolized in Beelzebub = the Lord of the Flies) and even with the future of mankind.

Thus the island adventure book becomes a fable of the possible development of human nature, a parable of the fall of man.

In a collection of essays, *The Hot Gates* (Faber and Faber, London 1965) Golding included a lecture he had given in America in 1962, under the title 'Fable'. In it he answers "some of the standard questions which students were asking" him about *LoF.*

"... The fabulist is a moralist. He cannot make a story without a human lesson tucked away in it. Arranging his signs as he does, he reaches, not profundity on many levels, but what you would expect from signs, that is overt significance. By the nature of his craft then, the fabulist is didactic, desires to inculcate a moral lesson. People do not much like moral lessons. The pill has to be sugared, has to be witty or entertaining, or engaging in some way or another ... If the pill is not sufficiently sugared it will not be swallowed. If the moral is terrible enough he will be regarded as inhuman; and if the edge of his parable cuts deeply enough, he will be crucified."

Later on, he says:

"Man is a fallen being. He is gripped by original sin. His nature is sinful and his state perilous. ... I looked round me for some convenient form in which this thesis might be worked out, and found it in the play of children. I was well situated for this, since at the time I was teaching them. Moreover I am a son, brother, father. I have lived for many years with small boys, and understand and know them with awful precision. I decided to take the literary convention of boys on an island, only make them real boys instead of paper cutouts with no life in them; and try to show how the shape of the society they evolved would be conditioned by their diseased, their fallen nature." ('Fable', p. 85 and p. 88)

Golding also explains that the theme of his book is

"an attempt to trace the defects in society back to the defects of human nature. The moral is that the shape of society must depend on the ethical nature of the individual and not on any political system ..." (quoted in E. L. Epstein, "Notes on W. Golding and Pincher Martin", Capricorn Edition of *LoF,* p. 250)

Peter Brook's famous film version of *Lord of the Flies* is a sensitive rendering of Golding's novel; it sticks closely to the book as far as the dialogue is concerned and contains superb portrayals of the characters of Ralph, Piggy and Jack. Simon's confrontation with the pig's head on a stick has, however, been omitted so that Simon's character does not come out quite as clearly. The very end of the film (with its magnificent camera work) departs from the book in so far as no word is spoken between Ralph and the naval officer; the camera 'holds' on Percival's eloquent silence.

## Methodology

*– Structuring the novel*

A clear outline and consistent structuring of the whole novel is vital for the teacher to know and keep track of his course. Therefore, on pp. 15 to 18 an outline of the twelve chapters of the novel is given, with subdivision into smaller units which are numbered, a, b, c and so on. This allows immediate orientation regarding the point reached in the analysis of the novel. In addition, those passages are marked that should be dealt with in close reading and intensive classroom discussion.

*– Time planning*

The unit as suggested in the Stundenblätter requires twenty teaching hours, which seems an adequate amount of time to devote to this novel. Students tend to lose interest if a unit goes on for too long. Admittedly, some of the lessons outlined in the Stundenblätter demand a great degree of concentration and might easily be expanded into a double period. On the other hand, some lessons could also be condensed, and thus time be saved (e.g. by dealing faster with chapters 3, 5 and 10 in a Grundkurs). The structuring of the whole unit should serve as an orientation for the teacher's individual time plànning; ultimately, the students' interest and motivation will determine how many additional lessons might be included, or, conversely, how much the plan ought to be condensed by covering parts of some chapters relatively quickly with student or teacher "summaries".

*– Technical suggestions*

Certain technicalities must be clarified right at the beginning to ensure an unhampered classroom procedure and thus save time for an engaged and concentrated discussion of the plot as it develops, and its meaning.

1. The students should be informed about the methodological approach taken towards Golding's novel. This means that they are instructed about the division of the twelve chapters of *LoF* into four main parts of three chapters each, and of the further subdivisions, which must be numbered. (To begin with, these are dictated by the teacher and noted down in the students' copies; later on, the students may learn to subdivide a chapter into several parts themselves.)
2. They should be told *how* to read this novel; i.e. the difference between extensive reading for gist, and intensive reading for detail must be explained. The students must be prepared for reading longer passages than they might be used to. They should know how much to read at one sitting, and how to go about it. They should be encouraged to underline (in different

colours!) anything that strikes them as important with regard to characterizations, setting, symbolism, theme, etc. Also they should be encouraged to write down their spontaneous reactions and comments whenever possible.

3. Within the context of "extensive reading" the students should be told that one of our teaching goals is their enjoyment of the novel, and that therefore they should read longer passages without reference to a dictionary. On the other hand, however, there are a number of terms and phrases in the text that simply require a brief explanation (e.g. "the Home Counties", "chapter chorister boy", and a good deal of schoolboy slang). In addition, it is only fair to state that Golding frequently has a somewhat extravagant choice of words in his descriptive passages, which makes reading difficult sometimes. To save the students time and to encourage their fluent, cursory reading, a list of annotations and explanations of hard words should be handed out in the first lesson. (Worksheet, p. 126ff.) As a rule, the words on this list need not be learned.
These annotations (approximately 500 items) do not contain explanations of all unknown or difficult words, but only of phrases and pieces of information that are important for an unimpeded understanding of the text. Thus a certain guarantee is given that the students know the contents well enough to be able to talk about the novel, even though there probably remains a certain number of unknown words whose meaning must be guessed from the context.
Only when the students reach those passages in the text which the teacher designates for close reading, or rereading, will they need to refer to a dictionary. These pages are to be read and prepared intensively; any unknown words should be looked up and written down in a separate word list.

4. The students should know that they have a "standing" homework, not to be repeated 'expressis verbis' by the teacher after each lesson: a written summary of the contents of every part in a few words or sentences, or a kind of headline for it. In this way they learn to distinguish essential from less important information, and to summarize the gist of a passage. This should be done on special pages so that eventually they have a brief outline of the whole plot of the novel, which makes for easier reference when needed.

5. In order to direct their attention to important developments or points worth discussing the students will be given "guiding questions" along with their homework of reading and preparing the chapters. Whether these should be answered in writing or just considered a help in their preparation is up to the teacher to decide.

6. As a rule board diagrams are to be copied while they are being developed on the board or on the overhead projector.

7. The teacher must determine whether or not a summary ("protocol") of the lessons ought to be written in which the central points of discussion should be noted down. If this is decided on, the students must be instructed on the format and relevant details.

8. As regards the planning of student "assignments" (Referate), it may suffice at first to announce that the students will be offered some "assign-

ments" or "papers", in due course. However, it seems didactically and psychologically better to start reading the novel and to know more about it before any assignments are given.
Most of the suggested assignments, or 'papers' (cf. p. 111) should not be started until after the eighth lesson; and some not until after the 14th lesson as they require a consideration of the whole novel. There will not be enough time to have all the papers read out; the teacher will determine which papers should be included in the lessons.

9. As there is no line numbering in the Faber edition of *LoF* the students should be told how to make a book-mark with their own lines count on it. The oblong book-mark should be the same length as the page, and the 34 lines indicated by dashes and numbers every five lines, so that with the help of the book-mark any lines quoted can be found without delay.

– *Text analysis in class*

As in a staggered approach to reading Golding's *LoF* the students are required to read increasingly longer, coherent sequences of the novel, they will soon be able to trace pertinent themes and recurrent motifs, and discuss them within a wider perspective. *LoF* adheres to a chronological order of events, and this order must be followed in the analysis of the novel. The discussion of *LoF* will show that the construction of the book represents a process of gradual revelation. Although the ambivalence of certain characteristics of the island setting and of the boys' behaviour is present from the beginning it may go unnoticed at first, as long as the reader has not been alerted to some of the signals embedded in Golding's language. The more thoroughly the first part of *LoF* is analysed in class (initially with substantial help from the teacher) the easier it will be for students to arrive at their own findings and conclusions in the later parts; and perhaps they will be able to think of comparisons, or contrasts, with other literary texts or historic events they are familiar with.

The chronology of the gradual development of the boys' island society, their splitting up into two conflicting groups (representing two opposed socio-political life-styles) and their incredibly anarchic behaviour towards the end, reflects the actual theme of the novel: the cancerous growth of evil that lies incumbent in the human heart. This theme must be increasingly accentuated and traced in the most revealing passages of the book. The most interesting lessons in this respect will be the ones towards the end, when the climax of the whole devastating development has been reached and its meaning and possible consequences have been discussed.
But all sorts of abstractions, explanations, comparisons may be brought into the discussion at earlier stages as well. The students may come up with theological speculations (e.g. in connection with Simon's death), or they may offer psychological explanations for the boys' change in behaviour (possibly conjuring up Freud or Jung). A comparison of the island "politics" with European state forms (democratic versus totalitarian) may be drawn, and other abstractions may be brought in. While any such comments and contributions are certainly relevant, a comprehensive discussion of the "fall" of man, and the nature of evil, had best be left till the end of the novel.

Although the predominant method of interpreting *LoF* is bound to be the discussion in class, every effort must be made to achieve methodological variety and to try to get the students themselves involved as much as possible in an analysis of the focal points of interest of the parts dealt with. This can be achieved through a number of student projects, through quiet re-reading of certain passages in class with subsequent discussion, through pair work, language-analysis in group work, prepared student paper / student comment, "guided" and "open" questions, etc. Group work lends itself more to the second half of the unit than to the first.

In many instances certain passages – to be prepared intensively – will be referred to and analysed with special care (and provide the basis for the board diagram). They should be read out either before or in the course of the interpretation. Ideally (and time permitting!), all passages that are specially referred to in class should be read out before being analysed.

Starting from the assumption that a penetrating text analysis can only be achieved if a paraphrase of the text makes certain that the students have really understood what they have read, the teacher may want to corroborate this with some further questions, especially with regard to the passage assigned for close reading.

It goes without saying that paraphrase and interpretation will often go hand in hand. Another important feature of any text analysis in class is the accompanying board diagram, which should be developed as the lesson progresses. Paraphrased points worth noting are written down briefly, and then a deduction, comment, or interpreting term relating to those points should be found. While the paraphrasing part can be kept short, it shouldn't be left out completely as the board diagram would most likely lose in clarity.

Considering that writing board diagrams takes up time, a number of variations might be envisaged. Thus, it may prove advantageous to prepare part of the diagram on a transparency (e.g. by writing down some relevant quotes from the text), and have the students complete the rest in class during the discussion. – Another possibility is to develop a diagram on a transparency up to a certain point in class, and to complete or supplement it in a later session. And why not present a completely "prefabricated" transparency to the students at the end of a lesson and ask them to verbalize it in the light of the findings of that particular class? (In that case it would be feasible to hand out the mimeographed diagram afterwards to save them time copying it.)

The board diagrams suggested in the Stundenblätter have been printed rather explicitly, without the abbreviations possible on a board, to keep them clear and "readable". Whenever they seem too weighty the teacher can streamline them with abbreviations or by leaving out paraphrasing items.

# Plan of the Unit "Lord of the Flies"

Most of the twenty lessons of this unit are considered separately, one by one, even though there will frequently be double periods available in practice.

The lessons are approached systematically as follows:

The *Notes on Interpretation* point out relevant details to be "discovered" and interpreted in the text, and implicitly provide the answer to most of the questions suggested in the Stundenblätter. Although these notes do not primarily aim at an in-depth academic interpretation of Golding's *LoF* but have been written with the possible level of achievement of our German students in mind, they are nevertheless meant as a help for the teacher and thus necessarily go beyond what need be discussed in class.

(To facilitate reference to the parts of each chapter the *Notes on Interpretation* have been printed coherently, following the chapter-by-chapter development of the novel.)

*Didactic Considerations* stand at the beginning of each lesson, in which the main teaching goals are briefly outlined, and important developments and the focal points of interest are stressed.

The *Plan of the Lesson* contains pertinent methodological hints and suggestions for which there would not be room enough in the Stundenblätter. They are kept as concise as possible.

The format of the enclosed loose-leaf Stundenblätter has been devised deliberately without detailed methodological suggestions; each lesson is structured thematically into several phases, or "steps". These are listed in the first column, under the heading *Lesson Structure.* The second column *Form of Lesson / Teacher's Impulses* contains brief methodological clues in the headings (not meant to duplicate the suggestions in the *Plan of the Lesson* but rather to supplement them) and, above all, a great number of impulses and questions with which to guide the students through discussions as logically and consequently as possible. (Paraphrasing questions usually precede interpreting ones.) In the last column, *Possible Responses / Results,* clues are given as to what might be expected as an answer to the questions raised. (For more explicit formulations the *Notes on Interpretation* should be referred to.)

A good deal of consideration has gone into the suggested *Board Diagrams* which form an important part of the Stundenblätter. Needless to say, any of the diagrams may be altered, adapted, improved on at the teacher's and students' discretion.

| Chapter | Passage | Contents |
|---|---|---|
| **I** | | **The Sound of the Shell** |
| a | p.7, l.1 – p.10, l.30 | English schoolboys wrecked on a tropical island. Ralph and a fat boy. |
| b | p.10, l.31 – p.16, l.11 | Ralph and Piggy characterized. Description of the island setting, the platform and the lagoon. |
| c | p.16, l.12 – p.18, l.22 | The finding of the conch. |
| d | p.18, l.23 – p.20, l.26 | Following the summons of the conch more boys appear partly dressed in their school uniforms. |
| e | p.20, l.27 – p.23, l.25 | Jack Merridew and his choir boys arrive. The first meeting. |
| f | p.23, l.26 – p.25, l.17 | The boys vote for Ralph as chief; Jack and his choir become hunters. |
| g | p.25, l.18 – p.32, l.6 | Ralph, Jack and Simon go on an expedition to explore the island. |
| h | p.32, l.7 – p.34, end | The piglet episode. Jack cannot make himself kill a small piglet. |
| **II** | | **Fire on the Mountain** |
| a | p.35, l.1 – p.38, l.22 | The second meeting. Ralph's report. Discussion of the boys' need of hunters and of rules. |
| b | p.38, l.23 – p.40, l.31 | Interruption by a little boy who claims to have seen a "beastie", a "snake-thing". |
| c | p.40, l.32 – p.42, l.26 | Ralph points out the need of a signal fire on the mountain. |
| d | p.42, l.27 – p.44, l.3 | The boys build a pile of wood. Jack and Ralph share a burden. |
| e | p.44, l.4 – p.47, l.34 | The fire is lit with a lens of Piggy's glasses. The boys debate and agree on more rules. |
| f | p.48, l.1 – p.51, end | The fire rages out of control. A little boy is missing. |
| **III** | | **Huts on the Beach** |
| a | p.52, l.1 – p.54, l.3 | Jack goes hunting, tracking a pig. |
| b | p.54, l.3 – p.60, l.16 | Ralph and Simon try to build shelters. |
| c | p.60, l.17 – p.62, end | Simon wanders off into the forest and finds a secret place of his own. |

| | | |
|---|---|---|
| **IV** | | **Painted Faces and Long Hair** |
| a | p. 63, l. 1 – p. 65, l. 6 | The rhythm of the children's island life. "Biguns"/ "littluns". Daylight play vs. the menace of the dark. |
| b | p. 65, l. 7 – p. 68, l. 4 | The destruction of sandcastles. Roger throws stones at a littlun. |
| c | p. 68, l. 5 – p. 69, l. 30 | Jack's mask. |
| d | p. 69, l. 31 – p. 74, l. 16 | Ralph sights a ship, but Jack's boys let the signal fire go out. Missed chance of rescue. |
| e | p. 74, l. 17 – p. 79, l. 25 | The hunters return with their first kill; great tension between Ralph and Jack. Piggy's specs are broken. |
| f | p. 79, l. 26 – p. 82, end | The feast. The hunters re-enact their hunt. Beginning of ritual. |
| **V** | | **Beasts from Water** |
| a | p. 83, l. 1 – p. 85, l. 29 | Ralph prepares himself for the assembly, the boys' third meeting. |
| b | p. 85, l. 30 – p. 100, l. 25 | The assembly. Eight boys speak in turn. The assembly is broken up by Jack. |
| c | p. 100, l. 26 – p. 103, end | Ralph, Piggy and Simon after the broken-up assembly, helpless. |
| **VI** | | **Beasts from Air** |
| a | p. 104, l. 1 – p. 105, l. 13 | Air battle explosions in the night; a dead parachutist falls down onto the mountain top. |
| b | p. 105, l. 14 – p. 112, l. 33 | Sam and Eric's exaggerated report of the "beast" creates general fear at the fourth assembly. |
| c | p. 112, l. 34 – p. 119, end | Expedition to the other end of the island. No beast! The boys discover a "castle" of rocks, a natural fort. |
| **VII** | | **Shadows and Tall Trees** |
| a | p. 120, l. 1 – p. 123, l. 16 | Expedition to the mountain top. Ralph feels depressed and helpless. Simon understands. |
| b | p. 123, l. 17 – p. 124, l. 13 | Ralph's daydream of home. |
| c | p. 124, l. 14 – p. 127, l. 13 | Ralph participates in a pig hunt and in the ensuing "pig-dance". |
| d | p. 127, l. 14 – p. 133, l. 30 | Following the pig-run the boys climb the mountain at night, in search of the beast. |

| | | |
|---|---|---|
| e | p. 133, l. 31 – p. 136, end | Ralph, Jack and Roger find a bulging creature and run off in panic. |
| **VIII** | | **Gift for the Darkness** |
| a | p. 137, l. 1 – p. 141, l. 13 | The fifth meeting. Jack's unsuccessful attempt to overthrow Ralph's leadership. |
| b | p. 141, l. 14 – p. 146, l. 30 | Piggy suggests a fire on the beach. More and more boys desert Ralph to follow Jack. |
| c | p. 146, l. 31 – p. 151, l. 22 | Jack, now chief of his tribe, hunts and kills a sow, leaving the pig's head as a gift for the "beast". |
| d | p. 151, l. 23 – p. 152, l. 26 | Simon, witness of the slaughter, is face to face with the pig's head, the "Lord of the Flies". |
| e | p. 152, l. 27 – p. 157, l. 31 | Ralph's and Piggy's fire is raided by Jack, Maurice and Robert. The sixth meeting. |
| f | p. 157, l. 32 – p. 159, end | Simon's confrontation with the Lord of the Flies; his recognition of evil. |
| **IX** | | **A View to a Death** |
| a | p. 160, l. 1 – p. 162, l. 19 | Simon finds and frees the dead parachutist. He knows the "beast" is harmless and wants to tell the others. |
| b | p. 162, l. 20 – p. 163, l. 28 | Ralph and Piggy, bathing, are almost completely deserted by the other boys now. |
| c | p. 163, l. 29 – p. 169, l. 10 | Jack's feast. The dance and chant ritual in the thunderstorm. Simon's death. |
| d | p. 169, l. 11 – p. 170, end | Simon's dead body on the beach is carried away by the tide. |
| **X** | | **The Shell and the Glasses** |
| a | p. 171, l. 1 – p. 175, l. 15 | The next morning Ralph and Piggy, ashamed, are haunted by their memories of Simon's death. |
| b | p. 175, l. 16 – p. 178, l. 30 | Chief Jack's harsh rule at fortified Castle Rock. |
| c | p. 178, l. 31 – p. 186, end | Nightly attack on Ralph's and Piggy's shelter; Jack and his hunters steal Piggy's glasses. |
| **XI** | | **Castle Rock** |
| a | p. 187, l. 1 – p. 192, l. 4 | The seventh meeting: a tiny group. Decision to go to Castle Rock and claim Piggy's specs back. |
| b | p. 192, l. 5 – p. 198, l. 34 | Ralph's desperate attempt to summon a new assembly at Castle Rock results in two bitter fights with Jack. |

| | | |
|---|---|---|
| c | p. 199, l. 1 – p. 201, l. 17 | Piggy trying to appeal for sense is killed by a large rock sent down by Roger. The conch is also destroyed. Ralph flees. |
| d | p. 201, l. 18 – p. 201, end | Roger, torturer and executioner now, is about to torment Samneric for Jack. |
| **XII** | | **Cry of the Hunters** |
| a | p. 202, l. 1 – p. 204, l. 10 | Ralph hides in the jungle, terrified by his memory of Piggy's death. |
| b | p. 204, l. 11 – p. 205, l. 3 | Ralph's confrontation with the Lord of the Flies, and his violent response to it. |
| c | p. 205, l. 4 – p. 211, l. 14 | In the dark Ralph sneaks up to Castle Rock and talks to Samneric who belong to Jack's tribe now. |
| d | p. 211, l. 15 – p. 220, l. 34 | Ralph is systematically hunted, with spears, rocks and fire. He runs for his life. |
| e | p. 221, l. 1 – p. 223, end | Unexpected rescue by a British naval officer and his men. |

(shaded) passages designated for intensive discussion

# Notes on Interpretation

## Chapter I: The Sound of the Shell

*The Initial Situation: Creepers in Paradise (Ia)*

The first pages of the novel convey the whole glamour that is shed over the setting, as well as the discomfort that is inherent in the cause of the boys' presence on the island. Golding presents a mixture of physical reality and modern fairy tale. And he includes, unobtrusively and hardly noticeable as yet, a fabric of symbolism that will become increasingly clear in the course of the novel.

The book begins with an intensely vivid, realistically described scene: two boys in the heat of a tropical island jungle working their way through creepers and broken trunks towards a lagoon; a tall, fairhaired boy, and a very fat, short, bespectacled boy, both British, as becomes clear from the school sweater and grey shirt (= part of a school uniform) and from a reference to the Home Counties (i.e. the counties around London). The boys' first appearance on the scene is accompanied by jungle birds' "witch-like" cries, – an eerie opening fanfare to the adventures to come.

The fat boy has greater difficulties moving through the undergrowth than his companion; he gets caught up in the creepers and eventually comes out into the open space backwards like a hedgehog or a pig. The open space is a "long scar smashed into the jungle" leading down to the lagoon. What caused this "scar" with its fallen jagged trunks is explained in the boys' talk about the attack on their plane, the releasing and dropping of the passenger tube with the children in it, and about the plane going down in flames with the pilot in it. The scar has been smashed by the tube crashing down the mountain slope; man's missile has cut a wound into the wholeness of nature.

The boys' talk, apart from explaining the reason for their arrival on the island, informs the reader of the tragic background against which this island adventure must be seen: the outside world from which the children have been catapulted onto the coral island is a world at war.

How do the two respond to their new surroundings? The fat boy's first question is about "the man with the megaphone", (perhaps a man in control of the intended evacuation) but he gets no answer. Instead, the tall boy, with extreme delight, states his belief that they are on an island – without any grown-ups! At this, the fat boy looks "startled". Obviously, these two boys are not just different in appearance, but also in character. The fat boy shows concern for "all them other kids", for the pilot, and for those children who must still have been in the tube when it was dragged out to sea in a storm. The fair boy, however, does not seem to share this concern, is rather offhanded and only mildly interested. Apparently the fat boy is turning the events of the last hours over in his mind, is concerned with the thought of what may have become of the others, while the tall boy is overcome by the sheer "delight of a realized ambition" – a coral island, and no grown-ups. The fair-haired boy does not seem too impressed with the insistent rational comments of the worried plump boy at his heels. His dynamic and athletic movements contrast with the other boy's asthmatic hard breathing; and even the way he speaks distinguishes him from the fat boy who is probably a Cockney and speaks somewhat sloppily and incorrectly. (This and the boy's reference to his "auntie" invites speculations as to his less privileged family background.)

When the fat boy suddenly gets restless and quickly crouches down among the bushes overcome by diarrhoea from eating too much fruit, Ralph uses the opportunity to move on and to leave the fat boy behind. After Ralph (and the reader through Ralph's eyes) has taken in the beauty of the scenery, palm trees, forest, the scar; then the lagoon, a coral reef, the sea – he displays his total enchantment by kicking off his shoes, ripping off stockings and garters, pulling off his shirt, lugging off his shorts and pants until he stands naked and free, like Adam in paradise – not hemmed in any longer by the "snake-clasp" of his belt!

To Ralph the island appears like a dream come true, but in the enchanting description of the island with its tropical colours, there are also "decaying" and "skull-like" coconuts; the fruits cause diarrhoea, as if the bodies of the children were not made for this paradise.

We remember that it is due to the destructive forces of a war raging in the world outside that the boys are stranded on the island. The question is: what will they make of this unexpectedly found Eden? Will they proceed systematically as Robinson Crusoe did?

### *Ralph and Piggy (Ib)*

Standing by the water's edge, naked, patting a palm trunk, Ralph is described as "the fair boy": his athletic build, his bright excited eyes, the "mildness about his mouth and eyes that proclaimed no devil". Ralph is just over twelve years old, – not yet adolescent and yet child no more. Whenever he is characterized the word "delight" steals in, supporting the reader's first impression of a boy who is totally enchanted by his new surroundings. His excitement finds a great variety of expressions, physical as well as verbal, and ranges from playfully machine-gunning the fat boy (innocently, laughingly imitating the war games which the grown-ups play!) after "Piggy" has revealed his nickname, to exclaiming schoolboy terms of rapture ("Whizzoh!") – sounding "the bass strings of delight."

In contrast to Ralph's enchantment and dexterity, Piggy, the fat boy, appears rather over-cautious, insecure; he cannot swim, talks of his "auntie" all the time, has "ass-mar" (sic!) and is kept busy cleaning his thick glasses. Trying hard to get at least a minimum of recognition from Ralph, he yields the secret of his nickname, trusting that Ralph will keep it to himself. But Ralph's blissful superficiality makes him indulge in repeating the descriptive "Piggy", which henceforth will remain the fat boy's only name.

When Piggy is forced behind the bushes again by another attack of diarrhoea, Ralph takes a closer look around him; through his eyes the reader becomes familiar with the island landscape.

A flat rock stretching from the mountain, through the forest, across a "terrace" of coarse grass and the sandy beach right down to the lagoon provides a sort of natural platform, about four feet above sea level. Because of some palm trees on it, this raised platform offers shade and relative coolness; fallen trunks lend themselves as benches. On the other side of the platform there is a large natural swimming pool in the beach, separated from the lagoon by a sandbank and supplied with water only at high tide. There is even a rocky ledge to sit on, at the farther end.

Piggy sits on this ledge on his return; then, admiring Ralph diving in the pool he determinedly undresses too, tiptoes to the shallow side, proudly ventures in and sits down "up to his neck in water". However, for all his physical disadvantage and lack of dexterity, Piggy is anything but a fool. He keeps asking pertinent questions, until Ralph's off-handedness is shaken and his daydreams are disturbed. Piggy's concerned, rational attitude comes out more clearly now. When Ralph mentions his "Daddy" – a commander in the Navy – and voices his childish conviction that his dad will come and rescue them, Piggy is only momentarily subdued. (He cannot refer to a flashy picture of a father in commander's uniform, – his dad is dead, and he is too embarrassed to talk about his mum; his "auntie" seems to have made up for the absence of his parents with "ever so many sweets" from her sweet-shop.) How should Ralph's dad know where to find the children? Dissatisfied with Ralph's superficial explanation Piggy insists, reminding Ralph of "the atom bomb" that must have killed everyone at the airport. "They're all dead."

This remark adds information on the background, the world outside. The children were being evacuated from the scene of an atomic war in Europe when the accident happened.

Piggy forces Ralph to face the implications of their situation. He repeats, "They're all dead." Nobody knows where the boys are. "We may stay here till we die." At the word "die", at long last, Ralph shows a reaction. In spite of the great heat he finds putting on his grey shirt "strangely pleasing" after Piggy's "ill-omened talk", as if the school shirt with its reminiscence of classroom order, discipline and security could protect him from the chilling thoughts of possible death. Then Ralph lapses back into daydreaming, and again Piggy tries to instigate him into acitivity. But Ralph is distracted by his realisation that a dream has come true, that an "imagined . . . place" has leapt into real life; and Piggy's logic is lost on him.

*The Conch (Ic)*

Before the two can arrive at a decision Ralph finds a shell in the lagoon. The physical reality of disentangling the conch from the weeds and getting it out of the water, then the admiration of the exquisite beauty of the glistening shell, and finally Ralph's various attempts to blow it – the description of this scene is full of boyish enthusiasm and exuberance. Piggy recognizes the conch as something "ever so valuable", he suggests blowing it for a practical purpose, to call the other boys and gather them in one place and have a meeting. Ralph hardly listens to Piggy at first; to him the shell is a pretty "plaything", and, typically, he is mainly interested in finding out how to blow it. His first efforts, amusingly enough, produce awkward "farting noises". Ralph is no Triton who, in Greek mythology, uses the conch to stir or calm the seas! But then, following Piggy's instructions, he learns to blow the conch better. The man-made sound of the shell disturbs the island peace: birds flutter up, something squeals and runs into the undergrowth.

From this moment the conch that summons the other boys becomes a symbol of great importance. Although inexpertly blown at first, creating unpleasant, harsh, threatening noises, it comes to be respected as a symbol of authority. The sound of the shell stands for "the harshness of human self-assertion as well as the signal of human sociability; . . . the sound of irresponsibility and childishness as well as of forethought and intelligence; . . . the fragility of order as well as the impulse towards it." (Kinkead-Weekes, p. 19)

*Obeying the Call (Id)*

Conjured up by the sound of the shell more and more boys appear on the platform. First "the innocent Johnny" with his trousers hanging down (diarrhoea); then others, all dressed (more or less) in school uniforms, all of them in natural obedience to the boy with the "trumpet-thing", and to Piggy who tries to register their names. The two boys with the conch are respected in the same way as the "men with the megaphones" had been, which ominously links the conch with elements reminiscent of disturbed order and war.

The children are satisfied that something "purposeful" is being done. Surprisingly enough, the frightening experience of the tube-crash seems to have left no scars on the boys' consciousness.

Golding gives a colourful description of the children's clothes, their multi-coloured badges and school mottoes. He even mentions "stripes of colour in stockings and pullovers" (– a point worth noting, as the boys will soon discard their school clothing, and before long will have different "stripes of colour" on their bodies!) and then lists the shades of colours of their hair. Thus an impression of great individuality and variety of types is created; the boys represent a wide range of individual characters, "full of eyes" down to the "bullet-headed twins" Sam and Eric.

*Jack Merridew and his Choir Boys (Ie)*

The next group to arrive stands in stark contrast with the strongly individualised, colourful group of boys that has assembled around Ralph and Piggy so far. "Something dark" is approaching in the haze of the beach, then a "creature" emerges from the mirage whose "darkness" is made up of shadow and clothing. When seen clearly the "creature" turns out to be a group of choir boys in full length black cloaks, with black caps on their heads, controlled by a boy also dressed all in black. In spite of the heat they walk in two parallel lines and march in step as though they were coming down a church aisle, or walking in a school procession. The boy in control shouts orders at them and does not permit anyone to leave the strict formation. Then he himself energetically vaults onto the platform with his black cloak flying like the wings of a huge bat.

Blackness and strict authoritarian organization are the first impressions of the new arrivals. The boy whom the choir address by his last name, Merridew, has quick, alert movements.

From the start, a strong personality makes itself felt. Although of about the same age as Ralph and Piggy, Merridew is clearly a boy with determination and authority. His physique is described as "tall, thin, and bony", his freckled face as "ugly without silliness". He seems to be a temperamental boy with a tendency to get angry easily; he certainly intimidates Piggy with the "offhand authority" in his voice. He keeps ordering the choir boys about, only allowing them to sit down after one boy has fainted, and telling them to take off their garments (after the vote). Jack Merridew is a boy who knows his own mind, as Ralph senses immediately.

For a while Jack's questions and comments dominate the scene. When he learns that there are no grown-ups he remains unperturbed: "Then we'll have to look after ourselves." However, before any further rational procedure can be developed, Piggy distracts Jack and promptly becomes the centre of derision, as Ralph unthinkingly blurts out the fat boy's nickname, adding ridicule to offence after Jack's humiliating term "Fatty". Thus Piggy is momentarily made an outsider ("the boys were a closed circuit of sympathy with Piggy outside", p. 23, l.9); blushing with shame he grows "pink" like a piggy!

In the ensuing naming some of the other boys are described in outline: Simon, the pallid boy who fainted; Roger, a "slight, furtive boy"; Maurice, grinning; and others.

*The First Meeting: Voting for a Chief (If)*

When Ralph realizes that the boys ought to have a chief "to decide things", Jack, in natural, boyish arrogance claims the chieftainship for himself on account of his being chapter chorister and head boy, – "I can sing C sharp"! Reasoning such as this puts the gathering of the boys into perspective: little school boys who have not quite realized yet the implications of where they are, and who apply the schoolroom standards from back home to their new surroundings. Their voting becomes a game in imitation of grown-ups; the "toy of voting" is accepted in the same manner as the blowing of the conch trumpet was. The vote is won by Ralph, (against the drearily obedient choir who vote for their leader), unexpectedly perhaps because obviously Jack is much more the leader type, and all practical suggestions have come from Piggy. But if there is something irrational in the outcome of the vote, it is due to the fact that the children associate Ralph with the conch. Ralph is marked by a "stillness", by his "size and attractive appearance", but "most obscurely, yet most powerfully" he is "set apart" by the conch.

When the boys applaud their newly elected chief, Jack's reaction reveals that this is more than just a game, after all. Jack's blush of mortification, his violent starting up shows that to him the vote represents a quest for power, and he has lost! Ralph senses this and appeases Jack by letting him remain in charge of the choir. Jack's immediate impulse is most revealing, "They could be the army –" (the picture of the almost military formation at the group's arrival projects itself again) but Ralph mellows this down: "Or hunters –" With these prerogatives settled Ralph and Jack develop a "shy liking" for each other.

Thus the first steps towards a democratic order on the island are taken.

*The Expedition (Ig)*

Ralph's first decision: before organizing their lives to meet the challenge of survival they must find out if they really are on an island. Exploring is another exciting game for the boys. It is also a matter of privilege for those to be chosen to go on the expedition. Ralph picks Jack (an obvious choice) and Simon from the circle of boys. Simon seems to hold a special appeal although so far we don't know very much about him except that he sometimes has fits, is skinny and "vivid", and has long black, coarse hair. When Piggy wants to come along also, Jack scares everyone into silence when in a violent, threatening gesture he drives his sheath-knife into a trunk. The clumsy, fat boy is not wanted, he is treated as an outsider again, and it takes some intelligence on Ralph's part to calm Piggy down and busy him with taking all the boys' names.

The more difficult the three boys' advance uphill, the more delighted they are. They squeeze themselves along animal tracks (pig-runs!) and with shining eyes exclaim in enthusiasm; overcome by the intensity of their emotions they start some mock-fighting to express their joy, "a happy, heaving pile." (This expression of the boys' excitement and "communion" is worth noting in view of later developments.)

When the boys come nearer to the top of the mountain they are distracted from their purpose again, they cannot resist the temptation of pushing some large, loose rocks: another exciting game! The falling rock is like "the passage of an enraged monster" and smashes a deep hole into the forest, leaving a replica of the scar caused by the tube. But the three boys are unaware of this parallel, and react with amazed excitement at the destructive forces they have set free. "Like a bomb!"

The top of the mountain allows them a view over the topography of the island. The island is boat-shaped, with an almost detached rock at its furthest end "standing like a fort". There is a coral reef about a mile out, enclosing more than one side of the island; then the open sea. The foamy streaks along the reef give the boys the impression that their island "boat" is moving steadily backwards. The beach can be seen, the scar in the forest, the platform with "insect-like figures" moving near it. The boys take in the glamour of the island, the unspoilt beauty of flowers and butterflies, trees, rocks and beach: all this belongs to them now, like a dream come true. Again they have this feeling of communion. "They were lifted up: were friends."

*The Piglet Episode (Ih)*

On the other side of the mountain there is a much steeper drop to the sea; and there is no reef in the sea. A cool breeze blows up on their faces from that side – a premonition of things to happen later on. On their way down the boys realize their hunger. Examining some exotic bushes with waxen buds Simon reveals his imaginative, almost poetic mind. "Like candles. Candle bushes. Candle buds." Although Ralph interprets Simon's words into realistic terms, Jack responds "contemptuously", slashing at one with his knife, "we can't eat them. Come on." The beauty of the buds is lost on him, he is a utilitarian. Jack's interest is aroused, however, when the boys suddenly find a piglet caught up in the creepers. Jack's knife is out immediately and for a second his raised arm is frozen over the squealing piglet. A pause – just long enough to make clear to the boys "what an enormity the downward stroke would be." Jack's arm is held back by an invisible hand, by his upbringing, by the taboos of the civilisation he comes from. The raised arm, the flashing blade, the piglet's extreme terror: a scene of great intensity, relieved only when the pig tears itself loose and disappears. Their ashamed laughter shows how the boys feel at this moment. They know the reason for Jack's hesitation: "because of the enormity of the knife descending and cutting into living flesh; because of the unbearable blood."

*Summing Up: The First Chapter*

The whole first chapter resounds with the "strings of delight"; wonderful games are played under the best possible conditions in perfect surroundings, the island offers the boys everything they could ask for, and such contrasts of character as exist (for example between Ralph and Piggy, or Ralph and Jack, or Jack and Piggy, or Simon and the others) are only natural.

The boys behave like real children who

are suddenly without their parents. They are innocent and playful, as boys would be at an age when being engrossed in games means living in a world of their own. They start by facing the new experience as an exciting adventure. The island is endowed with the features of an earthly paradise.
However, there are some darker undertones in the glamour as well. The island's beauty and wholeness has been disturbed by the fall of the tube, the jungle has received a wound which has left a visible "scar"; and the boys' exultant exuberance adds another gash, leaves a second scar in the forest. The island's peace is also disturbed by the harsh and blaring noise of the shell that sends animals rushing off into the undergrowth. Moreover, there are deceptive mirages on the island which make the distinction between appearance and reality difficult. Black "bat-like creatures" turn out to be weary choir boys, for example. The island "boat" appears to be moving backwards. And there are further ambiguities which are not immediately palpable and yet make themselves felt: the strict marching formation of the choir has something of army precision about it, the head boy's control over his choir seems just a little too authoritarian, the black, "uniformed superiority" too suggestive. Ralph's "machine-gunning" Piggy, and, later, his knocking Simon down in a frenzy of delight, playful as it is, rekindles the reader's awareness of the war-background of the adult world.
The boys' games, the conch, the "toy of voting", the expedition with the rock-rolling, the piglet episode – are all authentically enjoyable and genuinely boyish, and yet at the same time perfectly ambiguous.

## Chapter II: Fire on the Mountain

*The Second Meeting: Ralph's Report (IIa)*

After their return from the expedition to the mountain top, Ralph reports their findings. The boys have, once again, followed the summons of the shell and sit roughly in a triangle in front of Ralph on the platform, a neatly ordered grouping reminiscent of British school debates. The platform provides an ideal place for parliamentary discussion. But Ralph's report is immediately interrupted by Jack's unrestrained comments concerning an "army" – for hunting pigs. "All three of them" get carried away for a moment by the memories of the excitement of the piglet episode, and Jack wildly slashing his knife into a trunk promises that "next time" the pig won't get away. Ralph settles the boys down again. After stating the facts (the island is uninhabited, there are pigs, no grown-ups) he draws the appropriate conclusions: the boys will have to look after themselves. This means a self-reliant organization of island life. The boys will indeed need hunters to get them food, so Ralph can accept Jack's suggestion; and they need certain basic rules to organize their proceedings. Learning from the experience of this meeting Ralph suggests having "hands up" as at school, and only he who holds the conch is permitted to speak. The conch thus gains in importance, it is not only the signal horn (cf. "trumpet-thing", megaphone) but also a symbol of authority, of the right to speak, an instrument of democratic order.
But there is a sinister touch about Jack's enthusiastic support of "lots of rules": he interrupts Ralph again, thus disobeying the very rules just agreed on, only to express his eagerness to inflict punishment if anyone breaks these rules! While

Ralph is making a rational attempt to guarantee a functioning order of the boys' community, Jack thinks in terms of threats and violence.
At that, Piggy plucks up courage and takes the conch from Ralph; his concern is greater than his timidity and he criticizes Jack for hindering Ralph and "not letting him get to the most important thing" – rescue. Against Jack's irrational and instinctive outburst Piggy now sets logical analysis of the situation, pointing to the direction which the discussion should take. "Nobody knows where we are."
This is enough prompting for Ralph to take over again. He repeats Piggy's words, and adds, twice, "We may be here a long time."
For a moment the boys are silent, a cool breeze touches their faces and they seem worried. But then Ralph's light-hearted exuberance breaks through again: what is the good of worrying if this is such a "good island" with "food and drink" and (again, much to Piggy's dismay, Jack and Simon interrupt, adding:) "rocks" (Jack!), "blue flowers" (Simon!).
Ralph in his easy-going optimism feels that they can have "a good time" on the island. It will be as in those well-known island adventure books that the boys mention. This optimistic tenor ("good time / our island / good island / we'll have fun until the grown-ups come to fetch us") completely overrules the concern and silence provoked by Piggy's words. In the end Jack asks for the conch, for the first time obeying the new rule, and sums up the superb qualities of the island: there is food, water, – "everything".

*The "Beastie" (IIb)*

An unexpected gloom is cast on the optimistic and cheerful mood when a little boy with a mulberry-coloured birthmark claims to have seen a "snake thing" in the woods, a "beastie". Ralph tries to laugh this off at first, and to explain away the little boy's fear with dreams, nightmares. But his rationalization is ineffective; Piggy, interpreting the little boy's whispered words, keeps on and on, until Ralph gets exasperated, repeating "But there isn't a beastie!" Jack interferes, making matters worse, saying they would hunt the snake, if there was one. In the end Ralph feels helpless; five times he has had to repeat that there *is* no beast or snake on the island. ("It's a *good* island!") But the boys' laughter has died away, silence reigns, "something ungraspable" is in the air.
An irrational element has intruded into the assembly and has chilled the buoyant gaiety of the meeting's beginning. A "snake", product of the little boy's fearful imagination at work in the dark, has been released into the boys' earthly paradise. It reminds the reader of the snake in the Biblical paradise that tempted Adam into sin and made him fall.

*The Need of a Signal Fire (IIc)*

The momentarily depressed atmosphere is lightened again when Ralph remembers "the most important thing" (Piggy's words taken up again!) that he has to speak about: rescue. Bridging the gap between the boys' desire for fun and good times and their newly kindled indefinable fear, Ralph states, in simple terms, that they want both to have fun *and* to be rescued. These words bring him passionate applause and generate a new sense of community. Rather childishly he tells the others of island maps that the Queen (!) has, and that, one day, his father, a Navy commander, will come to their rescue. Such naive statements show Ralph's ignorance; he does not seem to realize

that there are innumerable unmapped islands, and his childish faith in the adult world of Navy and Queen falls in line with his adventure-book attitude towards life. – However, the conclusion he draws makes sense: the boys must send out smoke signals, they need a signal fire on the mountain. Fire represents hope; Ralph is confident that the signal will be seen and that the boys will be rescued.
Once the decision has been made, all the boyish excitement comes back with a vengeance; the rules are forgotten, the meeting breaks up without an organized ending. Everybody just rushes off to the mountain – following Jack, leaving Piggy and Ralph behind on the platform. Parliamentary democracy does not quite work yet, boyish ebullience is stronger. When Ralph runs off as well, a disappointed Piggy takes care of the conch, and, muttering to himself in disgust like a middle-aged father about that "crowd of kids", laboriously follows after.

*The Game of Preparing the Fire. (IId)*

An attentive reader will note a symbolic significance in the description of the "platform of forest" on the other side of the mountain where the boys gather their firewood (p. 43, l.1–3): the trees fall early and decay, because there is not enough fertile soil for full growth, and the new saplings make their way up through creepers. This corresponds to the description of the other platform, the boys' meeting place, where the palm trees too do not have enough soil to grow to any height (p. 12, l.25). Should this foreshadow the children's development on the island? They, like the saplings, will have to make their way through "creepers" (physical and mental); will their "soil" (their physical and moral substance) provide them with enough strength to grow and prosper?

Just as the boys' behaviour at the end of their second meeting displays the innocence of children as well as their irresponsibility, their building a pile of firewood reflects the same pattern. Again, getting the wood is an exciting game to them; the purpose for which they are gathering it or the problem of lighting the fire und maintaining it, is not at all on their minds.
Everyone takes part in this new enjoyment; everyone is busy collecting wood for the pile (except Piggy). Community action is stressed: seven boys lay hand on one log and carry it to the top together. A little later Ralph and Jack, too, share a burden – "Together, joined in effort by the burden" they heave the log up, "together" they chant and laugh with triumphant pleasure. Their common effort leads to a sense of togetherness, a "strange invisible light of friendship, adventure and content" comparable to the "solemn communion of shining eyes" the boys had when exploring the island (p. 29, l.13).

*First Failures / More Rules (IIe)*

So engrossed are the boys in their dedication to building the pile that such practicalities as the question of how to light the fire never even occur to them. This shows how unconsidered their activities still are; they only think of the next step, not of the ones to follow. They don't put "first things first and then act properly" as Piggy disdainfully comments a little later on.
Overcome by his brilliant idea of using Piggy's specs as a burning-glass Jack snatches the specs from the fat boy's nose without even asking him. Piggy's "shriek of terror" at this sudden assault reflects the half blind boy's feelings; and, most revealingly, also, Piggy's almost simul-

taneous "You'll break the conch!" shows Piggy's constant concern about the fragile shell which he cherishes so much. Ralph too is mastered by excitement when he elbows the half-blind Piggy aside to get quick access to the pile of wood. There is general pushing and pulling while the children watch Ralph's efforts to kindle a flame. (Golding's poetic licence with regard to the lenses of Piggy's specs need not be commented on; nobody is likely to notice that sunrays cannot be focused with the concave lenses of glasses for somebody who is short-sighted.) The successful lighting of the fire results in renewed joy and excitement.

But once more it turns out that the boys have acted thoughtlessly; again they have neglected to think of the consequences of their actions. The fire doesn't produce any smoke and it burns down in no time. Disappointed and tired Ralph admits defeat, seconded by Piggy. Jack, who apparently reacts with nervous irritation whenever Piggy speaks up, derisively and contemptuously tells him to "shut up", and harshly overrules Piggy's feeble, twice repeated "I got the conch" with his comment that the conch doesn't count on the mountain. At that Ralph steps in. He seems to sense in Jack's words the danger of devaluing the significance and the power of the conch, and comes to Piggy's rescue indicating the need of more rules. Not only does he think of special guards for the fire, but he also maintains the supreme importance of the conch as a symbol of authority and the right to speak. "Where the conch is, that's a meeting." As all the boys agree this must be considered a new attempt at consolidating a reliable order among the boys. Jack's readiness to share responsibility comes out when he volunteers to have part of his choir / "hunters" maintain the fire, and another part keep watch to catch sight of a ship. This clear division of duties and acceptance of responsibilities constitutes a demonstration of faith in a democratically ordered society. The boys are trying "to do the right things" and surely none of them would doubt the truth of Jack's words, spoken in simple arrogance and naive conviction: that, after all, they are not savages, but English; and the English are best at everything!

Jack's natural self-confidence and his trust in British grit to win through is a reminder of the attitude which the boys in Ballantyne's 'Coral Island' display throughout; his words will take on a different ring, though, when remembered at a later stage in the novel.

### *Fire out of Control (IIf)*

While the setting sun suddenly makes the boys aware of "the end of light and warmth", announcing the uncanniness of the dark and causing gloomy thoughts, Ralph's reassuring words are meant to calm the boys. When Piggy ventures out to state his opinion, he is immediately shouted down by the others; the children just do not want to listen to the indignant fat boy's comments. And yet, unexpected by all, even by Ralph, they suddenly do listen to him, hushed, falling "still and silent" when they follow Piggy's gaze down the "unfriendly side" of the mountain. Piggy with his flashing glasses is the first to see what has come of their "small fire". Without their noticing it, the unattended fire has eaten its way downhill and now almost the whole mountain top is on fire. The power of the fire becomes stronger and more savage, until a large stretch of the forest is "savage with smoke and flame."

When Piggy repeats his bitter, reprimanding words "You got your 'small fire' all right" to the boys who are now shocked

Piggy : fire <-> ho

into silence and awe at the power they have liberated, it becomes clear that the fire has taken on a different meaning. What began as a playful cooperative effort to express the children's optimism and hope, and their belief in rescue, has inadvertently set free reckless, destructive, elemental forces.

The same power seems to appeal to something savage in Ralph himself too (p. 49, l.8), as he wildly tells Piggy to "shut up!", not only repeating Jack's abusive words but also disregarding Piggy's right to speak. But this time Piggy insists, hanging on to the conch.

Against the "drum-roll" noise of the fire Piggy voices his opinion that the boys ought to be "more careful", i.e. more considerate. In view of the behaviour the boys have displayed so far Piggy is scared – but Jack interrupts him with a disgusted and offensive "Yah – Fatty!" before Piggy can say what he is frightened of. It seems as though Piggy has seen something in the "hell" of the forest fire to make him scared of the consequences of the boys' thoughtless behaviour. Typically, it is Jack who interrupts; typically, too, Ralph is so distracted and fascinated by the spectacle of that "splendid" and at the same time "awful" sight that he is not even listening. The crowd of other children, however, laugh at Piggy. They don't realize that this boy who is half blind without his glasses is in fact the only one to see clearly, to think rationally, and to make realistic suggestions. Like a scornful parent he says that they should have "put first things first" and built shelters instead of running up the mountain "like a pack of kids" (cf. p. 42, l.20) and making a useless "bonfire".

Piggy's words carry conviction, and the boys listen to him now. He has worked himself up into a frenzy and pours forth a real tirade, looking ahead to what might happen if the boys don't start displaying greater responsibility. Piggy is drawing consequences from their present experience; his question "Won't we look funny if the whole island burns up?" implies a serious warning, almost a premonition of the potential of savage power that lies dormant in the boys.

Piggy also shows his sense of responsibility by drawing attention to the little ones: they should not have been allowed to wander around wherever they pleased. And it is Piggy who notices that the little boy with the mulberry mark is missing, the one who talked about the "beastie". He was last seen "down there", where the fire is raging, and where a tree explodes "like a bomb"! The expression is a repetition of the phrase used to describe the destructive force set free by the rock which was released by the boys on their "expedition" and smashed a scar into the forest (p. 30, l.19). The deadly silence of the crowd is shattered when the little ones – apparently remembering the mulberry-marked boy's "snakething" story – interpret burning creepers as "snakes" and start screaming.

Piggy – terrified by the only possible conclusion, repeatedly asks for the missing boy. His recognition of the truth makes his knees give. Piggy's fright and Ralph's shame make clear what the boys dare not admit openly: their inconsiderate and irresponsible behaviour has resulted in the loss of a child's life. There is a first victim on the island. Part of the island paradise has been destroyed; "snakes" have intruded. The "drum-roll" noise of the fire is an unpleasant, threatening sound, somewhat like the "farting noise" of the conch when first inexpertly blown. – There is a threat of evil in this scene, fear and confusion make themselves felt among the children. Clearly then, this fire should be a warning to the boys to be

reason

a threat
fear / confusion have intruded
destruction

more careful; Piggy has grasped the idea, most likely Ralph has too, but what about the others?

## Chapter III: Huts on the Beach

*Jack – the Hunter (IIIa)*

The description of Jack hunting in the jungle is of great intensity. Almost naked, on all fours, his nose nearly on the ground like a hunting-dog sniffing the scent, Jack is tracing the pigs' hoof marks following any such clues as broken twigs or polished plants, crouching, stealing forward, stopping ... He is holding his self-made weapon, a sharpened stick, in his hand, is breathing with flared nostrils like an animal, and stares into the dark undergrowth with "nearly mad" eyes: a picture of compulsion to track down and kill. The transformation of the chapter chorister boy into the passionate hunter is fearfully convincing.

The intensity of the scene is underlined by the silence accompanying it. Jack finds this silence oppressive, and is startled when he unwittingly disturbs a jungle-bird from its primitive nest of sticks (!) and provokes its harsh cry, which seems to come "out of the abyss of ages" (cf. the "witch-like cry" of the bird in the opening passage of chapter I.) Only much later in the book will it become clear that almost every word here is charged with symbolic meaning. The witch-like, devilish cries symbolize the dissonance of evil that forever disturbs the harmony of existence, as it has done since time began.

When Jack's nostrils catch the scent of pig's droppings he becomes wildly excited. Obviously, Jack has rediscovered in himself the hunting instincts that lie dormant in man; he seems to find it easy to revert to this natural state of primitive man. When his spear misses, and the pig escapes, Jack's swearing gives expression to his maddening disappointment and frustration.

*Ralph and Simon – the Home-builders (IIIb)*

On Jack's return to the terrace the intensity he displayed when hunting is paralleled by Ralph's concentration on the construction of the shelter he is trying to build with Simon's help. (Typically, Ralph is holding branches in his hand; Jack, a spear!) Here, too, the result is frustration; the hut is no more than a "wreck". Two shaky shelters is all they have managed in days, as they have been deserted by all the other kids who prefer playing and swimming to constructive work. Ralph sounds bitter. He knows they'll "never get it done." Even while he is talking to Jack the hut collapses and Ralph gives up for the moment. Democracy and civilisation don't function yet.

The conversation of the two boys reveals the growing antagonism between Jack the hunter and Ralph the home-builder. Jack's "We want meat" stands against Ralph's "We want shelters". Disappointed by the selfishness of the other children, Ralph tries to convince Jack of the need of shelters. Jack, the hunter, for his part tries to "convey the compulsion ... that was swallowing him up". He just "had to go on", thinking he might kill a pig. Jack's reactions here as in many other parts of the book are fierce, hot-headed, selfish. He is easily enraged, his face is "flushed", or "rapt". Ralph, although more reserved, also finds it hard to keep his "hidden passions" down and only to allow "untertones" in his voice to betray his indignation.

Ralph shows his sense of social responsibility when he explains that places are needed that are safe in storms, and – more important – "a sort of home" is needed for the little ones who have nightmares and scream "as if the snakething was real", as Simon is outspoken enough to say. Ralph does not admit any fear of his own, but both he and Jack "flinch" when Simon mentions the "beastie"; and Jack is prompted to speak of the strange feeling he sometimes has when he is on his own, hunting: "as if something's behind you all the time in the jungle"! So he knows how the frightened little ones feel at night.

Ralph's primary concern is building shelters, maintaining the fire, and above all, rescue. Jack, however, has almost forgotten what 'rescue' is, so obsessed is he with his hunting instinct. The mad look gets into his eyes again, that counter-agent to reason. All he can think about now is how to steal up to a pig, "paint our faces so they wouldn't see ...", whilst Ralph is talking about smoke signals to attract ships ... When Ralph shouts indignantly "Don't you want to be rescued?" Jack only repeats that they want meat. He claims that his hunting is work, too; but Ralph knows that Jack *likes* his work, *enjoys* hunting, *wants* it. Ralph is trying to fulfil a duty, to live up to his responsibility for the others, while Jack is satisfying his personal drives and instincts.

They look at each other "baffled", "two continents of experience and feeling, unable to communicate."

*Simon – the Mystic (IIIc)*

Simon is entirely different from both Jack and Ralph. In a way he, like Piggy, is an outsider. His occasional fits make him the object of Jack's derision; he is rather shy, and even Ralph thinks Simon is "queer" and "funny". But Ralph likes Simon because he is unselfish, helps in building the shelters and is "always about". Also, Simon is the one to protect Piggy against Jack (p. 46, l.17).

In IIIc Simon is characterized as vividly as Jack is in IIIa; in fact, the two passages show a certain amount of parallelism and contrast. In both there is a mixture of direct description and indirect characterization through the boys' behaviour and their reaction to their surroundings.

Simon's outward appearance contrasts with that of the red-haired and freckled Jack. He is small and skinny, "always darkish in colour", has long black hair; there is something foreign about him. His eyes are extremely "bright", contrasting with Jack's "mad" looking eyes. Like Jack Simon is barefooted, like him he walks through the jungle alone.

However, before Simon worms his way into the intricacies of the undergrowth, he is depicted at the beach, and then among the children under the fruit trees. When Simon frowns at the little ones' uncompleted "hut" in the sand this shows his concern at the fact that even in their games the children leave a job unfinished, mirroring Ralph's unsuccessful efforts with the shelters. His sense of social responsibility is evident, indicating an affinity to Ralph and Piggy. The picture of Simon walking through the fields of fruit trees where flower and fruit grow together on the same tree is most suggestive, this and the humming of "bees at pasture" suggests a perfectly harmonious and peaceful, paradisiac scene.

It is after this memorable scene that Simon moves on into the darkness of the jungle. The change in description is quite marked: dark air, pale flowers, shivering creepers, clamorous birds determine the atmosphere now. The island contains both Eden-like qualities and the dark, uncanny jungle with its creepers, "ropes", parasitic flowers and climbers, witch-like cries. But Simon is not scared at all; he is not beset by any fear of strange "beasts". He manages to find a place where sunshine falls through, a "bowl of heat and light", surrounded by dark but aromatic bushes.

The comparison with Jack offers itself again. Like Jack, Simon looks over his shoulder to make sure he is all alone in the jungle, – "utterly alone"; like Jack (p. 53, l.9) he is almost "furtive" for a moment. But while Jack has to admit that he feels "hunted", as if "something" was behind him all the time (p. 57, l.26) Simon enjoys his solitude, and feels "secure" in his little cabin from which he can overlook the clearing with the butterflies dancing in the air. Like Jack he "cocks a critical ear" at the island sounds, but he hears all the concerted noises (bees, birds, the sea), and they do not scare him. And when the "honey-coloured sunlight" gives way to thickening darkness (– the almost Shakespearean metaphorical language in this passage underlines the exquisite beauty of the scene –) Simon takes in the wonder of the starlit jungle night with all his senses: the opening nightflower "candle-buds", the scent they spill. This is what distinguishes Simon from Jack, the hunter, the utilitarian, who slashes the useless "candle-buds" with his knife, but whose heart beats faster at the sight of steaming pigs' droppings.

Simon seems to be in solitary communion with nature, and in perfect peace. He is the first boy to realize what the island and the jungle are like in themselves; he registers and accepts the two sides of the island reality. He has the eyes to see the daylight reality of the island, but also to recognize the unspeakable beauty of the night. His sensitivity allows him to know intuitively and comprehensively.

Maybe it is yet too early to state that there is something indescribably "Christian" about Simon, that he has something of a mystic, or even a saint, as Golding himself once remarked in an interview.

## Chapter IV: Painted Faces and Long Hair

### *The Rhythm of Island Life (IVa)*

Chapter IV is carefully constructed in itself. Starting with the revealing description of the regular rhythm of the boys' island life Golding turns his attention to the "little ones" and observes their behaviour, before returning to the bigger boys.

The daily rhythm of the children's life on the island is the slow pendulum swing from bright, happy mornings, when play is good and life full of excitement, to the heat of noon and the mirages and illusions of midday, when the sun gazes down on them "like an angry eye", and on to menacing dusk with its threat of darkness that comes "like an extinguisher" and makes the children crawl fearfully into their shelters. While they completely ignore the "snapping sharks" waiting on the other side of the reef in the distance, the sudden fall of darkness and the anticipation of nightmares makes them restless . . .

The division of the boys into the two categories "littluns" and "biguns" may be taken as just the expression of a natural border line between different age groups; it might however also be understood as a sign of the bigger boys' selfish concern not to be bothered with the smaller children. So the "biguns" play their games of "hunting", "exploring", "fishing", etc, whilst the "littluns" busy themselves with aimless and trivial play, leading a life entirely of their own. They build sandcastles which they decorate with "interesting stones" (!); they draw marks, tracks, railway lines in the sand and create their own imaginative world.

*Sand and Stone Throwing (IVb)*

In a convincingly real sequence of situations Golding illustrates the irrationality of violence and thus comments on basic elements of human nature.
While three of the littluns are kneeling in the sand playing peacefully and with absorbed attention, two biguns, Roger and Maurice, walk right through their sandcastles, laughingly destroying the tracks, walls, and railway lines, and scattering the flowers and chosen stones. When Percival starts crying because Maurice has kicked sand into his eye, Maurice runs off quickly, remembering a punishment for a similar offence "in his other life". He feels the "unease of wrong-doing", is still conditioned by the memory of a parent's "heavy hand"; although this memory is obviously not strong enough to prevent him from doing such an act of senseless destruction in the first place!
No sooner has Maurice disappeared when the smallest boy on the island, the six year old "innocent" Johnny (cf. p. 19, l.25) whose "natural belligerence" has been mentioned in passing (p. 65, l.18), watches Percival and suddenly flings sand into his face, making him cry again. Clearly, little Johnny is too young to have been conditioned by his parents, or 'society'. He just gives in to his innate belligerent instinct triggered off by the bigun's example. Even after Percival has run off crying, Johnny keeps on throwing sand at his imaginary playmate!
Meanwhile little Henry is poking about with a white stick trying to control the motions of tiny scavenging creatures on the beach. Again, a small child's game turns into something more irrationally meaningful: the six year old boy feels that he has control over living things! He has the "illusion of mastery" and enjoys this sensation "beyond mere happiness"!
All this while little Henry himself is being watched by Roger, who stands hidden behind a palm tree and whose "gloomy" and "forbidding" face predicts no good. The sudden fall of big coconuts that could have killed Roger had he been hit, gives him an idea. He picks up a stone, then a handful of stones, and in an act of inexplicable violence starts throwing them at Henry – but aiming to miss. Thus Roger, too, is exercising control over a living being, and enjoying this sensation, the "illusion of mastery" when Henry obediently turns this side and that. But he is older than the littluns; he is acting deliberately and seems to be playing with the idea of actually hitting and hurting the child. Why else should he jump back behind the palm tree "breathing quickly, his eyelids fluttering" when Henry innocently comes looking for the "friend" teasing him?
What lies dormant in Johnny's belligerent impulse, and in Henry's enjoyment of his control over living creatures, comes to the fore in Maurice's aggressiveness and reveals itself most frighteningly in Roger's stone throwing.
But Roger does not dare to hit Henry. Like Maurice he is restrained by "the taboo of the old life", by the memory of "parents, school, policemen, the law", i.e. the civilization the boys come from and according to whose standards they have been educated. ("Taboo" here stands for "rules", "principles", "commandments".) Their urge towards violent behaviour is restrained by their social conditioning, not by something in their own nature.

But we remember that this very civilization has proved frail and lies in ruins now and cannot reinforce the social taboos. There are no parents, schools, policemen to guide the children! Their civilization has broken down because its morality was not strong enough to prevent men throwing atom bombs at each other. Man's aggressive and destructive nature has proved stronger. It is only natural then that before long the boys will remember devices used by the adults in their warfare (such as camouflage) behind which to hide their shame.
Little Henry and the belligerent Johnny, however, will unite and continue to throw sand at Percival, oblivious of the goings-on around them (p. 73, l.7).

### *Liberation through Camouflage: Jack's Mask (IVc)*

Significantly, Roger is called away from his ambush by Jack, who is too eager and impatient to notice the blushing that reveals Roger's bad conscience with regard to Henry. Jack tells him of his idea to paint his face so that the pigs would not see him when he was creeping up on them. His excitement and compulsion come out again in his twisting "in the urgency of telling". Typically, Jack draws on the experience from one particular aspect of their societal background, but it is not the background of school or church; he remembers the dazzle paint as used to conceal soldiers, cars, ships in the war. "Things trying to look like something else."
Roger understands. His grave nodding signals that he is on the same wavelength as Jack. (The concealing paint would hide the "darker shadow" of shameful blushing, too.)
The effect of Jack's painted face on the other boys as well as on Jack himself becomes apparent immediately: the twins are intimidated, and Jack's tone becomes bossy, imperative. However, he is not satisfied until he has made his face even wilder, slashing a thick, black charcoal line across, turning himself into an "awesome stranger". With excited laughter he welcomes his loss of identity; the freckled boy with his sandy eyebrows has disappeared behind the alienating and appalling mask. The mask becomes "a thing of its own" behind which Jack can hide; it frees him from "shame and selfconsciousness", i. e. from the taboos of the old life. The age-old function of the mask stemming from the "abyss of time" has here been remembered and brought to life again.
Again the boys' reaction is revealing: while Jack feels compelled to dance like a primitive native he seems to work himself up into a frenzy, his laughter becomes a "bloodthirsty snarling", and he forces the boys to form a line so that he can enact an imitation pig hunt. He is indeed "liberated", is beside himself, determined to go after the pigs with renewed courage and resolution. Jack's reversion to savagery has begun. His effect on the other boys is appalling, scaring them, making them fall silent and try to escape. But the mask compels them.

### *Abandoned Responsibilities: Missed Chance of Rescue (IVd)*

After the display of Jack's reversion to savage behaviour in IVc, the following passage when we see Ralph confronted with Piggy's matter-of-fact ideas represents a pronounced contrast.
Piggy's suggestion of using a stick for a sun-dial is meaningful in two respects: on the one hand it is indicative that Piggy thinks of putting a stick to a practical ("scientific") purpose (whilst Jack uses a

sharpened stick as a weapon, like his knife); on the other hand it shows Piggy's rather wearisome clinging to an entirely useless conventional "lunch time" / "tea time" routine which has long since been superseded by the new rhythm of island life.

Piggy's seriousness shows him as utterly devoid of any sense of humour; he is not only an "outsider" but also a bit of a bore. And yet it is Piggy's holding on to his memory of the world where Auntie's "lunch time and tea time" determined the rhythm of his life that makes him think of rescue all the time (something almost completely obliterated from Jack's mind). This insistence and constant reminder of "the most important thing" keeps pricking Ralph who feels "irked" by Piggy's remarks.

Piggy may be a bore, and he may be "clumsy", but he is also the most practical-minded boy on the island, and he is a realist. Piggy can think. When Ralph sights smoke on the horizon he and all the other boys fall into a frenzy of excitement and gaze out to sea as if hypnotized. Piggy is the only one to think logically and to turn round to see if there is a clear smoke signal on the mountain top to signal to the ship. Ralph cannot be distracted until Simon's outcry alerts him.

The mad race to the top of the mountain, once the fatal truth has been discovered, leaves Ralph shocked and frustrated at the sight of the dead fire when they get there. We remember Ralph's warning concerning the fire (p. 58, l. 9), but rescue, reason, common sense have proved less important to Jack and his boys than their hunting instincts. Ralph's agonizing frustration at finding that Jack's fire watchers have deserted their duties is made worse by the fact that a pile of unused fuel lies ready but cannot be put to use because by the time Piggy arrives it is too late to try and kindle a new fire. Ralph's heart-rending "Oh God, oh God!", and then his mad screaming "Come back! Come back!" at the ship disappearing on the horizon, reveals his helplessness and despair.

Ominously, Ralph is looking down "the unfriendly side of the mountain" when, just at that moment, the "hunters" return.

*Growing Antagonism / Broken Glasses (IVe)*

This is the most dramatic scene so far, a first culmination of the antagonism that has gradually built up between Ralph and Jack. The coinciding of Ralph's moment of tragic despair at the missed chance of rescue with the return of the hunters in their elated feeling of triumph at their first kill, adds poignancy to the situation. The hunters approach from the "unfriendly side" of the mountain; their "procession" is a strong reminder of Jack's group's first appearance (cf. p. 20!). But this procession now shows how much the boys have changed: they still wear their black caps but otherwise they are almost naked (having discarded their choir boys' gowns with the silver crosses). They still seem to be walking in step, as at the beginning, but now they lift sticks (!) in the air rhythmically, emphasizing the words they chant. The description makes us think of some native tribe rather than of little schoolboys, the more so when the "gutted carcass of a pig" is described as swinging from a stake which the hunters carry. We can guess with whose knife the pig's neck has been cut open: Jack's arm, once suspended in the air with the flashing blade (p. 33, l. 19) because of the "enormity the downward stroke would be" has now descended and cut into living flesh. The hunters are united in the regular rhythm of their chant ("Kill . . . Cut . . . Spill . . .")

drumming out the three monosyllables in threefold variation.

Excited, with lifted stick (now called "spear"), grinning, Jack reports their first kill. The "ecstatic grin" on the twins' faces reflects the hunters' enthusiasm. Again and again Jack gets carried away by the memory of their pig hunt; however, there are indications that show how unaccustomed to slaughter he is as yet. His grimacing "distastefully" at his blood-smeared hands (cf. "the unbearable blood", p. 34, l. 3!), his twitching when he proudly states that it was he who cut the pig's throat, his shuddering when he remembers the "lashings of blood", – all this indicates that he is not quite as brazen as his laughter seems to suggest.

Just the same, he wants to go hunting "every day" now: he has licked blood, his hunting instincts have found their first fulfilment, yet ask for more. Typically Jack starts cutting a notch in the handle of his knife to record the number of his killings (apparently in imitation of war-film heroes). Jack's ecstatic behaviour is portentously counterpoised by Ralph's unresponsive, dead serious face and the "sombre silence" of his group of four, who stand there motionless. But Ralph's repeated "You let the fire out" causes only a temporary uneasiness in Jack; the routine duty of keeping up a fire is a mere irrelevance to him in comparison with the profound pleasure to be had in killing a pig. While he is conscious of a fault, his consciousness is immediately obliterated by his memories of their struggle with "a living being", imposing their will on it (a feeling similar to little Henry's happiness at exercising control over living things, p. 66, l. 30!), killing it and enjoying the kill "like a long satisfying drink." Again, Jack recalls the blood; and as if aroused by the mere mention of blood his hunters begin to "buzz" excitedly, like a swarm of flies.

At this point, however, Ralph asserts his chieftainship. Tension rises as he takes a step towards Jack, authoritatively. His "There was a ship." is so charged with emotion and bitter reproach, and the implication is so obvious, that his words do not miss their effect; and the double repetition adds intensity and impact to the sentence. A chance of rescue has been lost because of the boys' irresponsible behaviour.

Jack's immediate reaction to Ralph's reprimand is to draw his knife and start cutting up the pig, thus finding an outlet for the aggressions that are building up inside him, the more so as Piggy cries out: "You and your blood, Jack Merridew!" But the intensity of Ralph's feeling allows for no interference from Piggy; he is facing Jack alone. His violent reproach causes Jack to stand up (threateningly?) and to counter with a half provocative, half excusing "We needed meat". Considering Jack's eagerness to hunt and kill, his argument seems feeble; most likely his compulsion is only disguising itself in the need for meat.

The crisis has come now as the two boys stand face to face, Jack with his bloodied knife in his hand, both in a state of extreme emotional tension. Jack's "brilliant world of hunting, tactics, fierce exhilaration, skill" in opposition to Ralph's "world of longing and baffled common sense". The high pitch of this dramatic scene provokes an act of violent behaviour when Piggy carried away by his bitterness makes another poignant remark. This is too much humiliation for Jack; all his accumulated aggression erupts when he plunges his fist into Piggy's stomach felling him like a pig and hits Piggy's head, breaking a lens of Piggy's glasses.

Unlike Ralph, whose frustration in this scene finds its expression in verbal reproach, Jack, typically, cannot restrain his anger and frustration and reverts to vicious physical violence, which he directs against the fat and helpless Piggy, whose comments provoke him beyond control. It is as though Jack's successful killing of a pig had liberated in him a destructive violence which he now applies to a human being; the first physical blow to be meted out to a boy on the island. Jack's violent behaviour results in Piggy's loss of one "eye": symbolically a partial destruction of clearsightedness and rationality by irresponsibility and viciousness and the beginning of a brutal chain of events that will lead to the much more devastating blow at Piggy's head that will kill him.

Although Ralph takes a step forward he cannot be challenged to interfere physically; Simon in never failing sympathy picks up the broken glasses and returns them to Piggy.

There is another moment of tension when Ralph does not want to accept Jack's apology, but instead calls it a dirty trick; a comment answered by a strange "opaque" light in Jack's eyes (cf. p. 58!) that clearly signals no good. In the end Ralph's silence wins him new respect as chief, but he and Jack are clearly "on different sides of a high barrier" now.

*The Feast: Beginning of Ritual (IVf)*

Roasting the pig over the newly-lit fire brings a relief of tension. The boys get back to normal again; the former circle of hunters is now a "circle of boys round a camp fire", hungry, concerned with nothing but food.

To Jack, however, who keeps hacking at the pig, this feast means a personal triumph: it was his hunting compulsion, cleverness and skill that got them the meat. Significantly, Jack is the "centre" of the circle of boys now, Piggy and Ralph are outside the circle, Ralph standing a few yards apart in the ashes of the signal fire (!) silently watching the others. His link with Jack is broken and has been transferred to Piggy.

Jack's raging attempt to convey to the others how much they depend on his cunning and courage does not have the expected effect though; in his rage he cannot express his feelings: he stutters, looks around for understanding, but finds only respect.

The embarrassing momentary silence is soon followed by frenzied excitement again, when the boys' memory of the pig-hunt is rekindled by Maurice, and they re-enact the hunt, forming a circle, dancing, chanting, pretending ... The transformation of the "camp fire" circle into something like a tribal circle doing a barbaric dance takes place almost instantly; the end of the tribe's rhythmic chanting is now even more brutal than before. ("Bash her in.")

This is the beginning of a primitive ritual. Like their smeared faces this ritual offers a mask behind which the boys can lose their identity, can feel liberated from their self-consciousness and from the shame at the enormity of their deed. The ritual constitutes a compensation for their shame and also for their fears.

Ralph's feeling of resentment as he watches the boys, silently, shows that he senses some danger in their behaviour. (But there is also something in Ralph that makes him feel envious of the boys' ecstatic ritual game!) His announcement of an assembly reveals his concern about the boys losing their self-control, about Jack's power growing and endangering such civilized projects as their building shelters or maintaining signal fires for their rescue. That is why he takes recourse to the conch and the parliamentary order it symbolizes.

## Chapter V: Beast from Water

*Ralph's Preparation for the Assembly (Va)*

As a result of his recent experiences Ralph has grown older. He realizes the need to think now and arrives at an understanding of the "wearisomeness of this life" (where one has to learn to "watch one's feet" to avoid falling); in comparison, their first day on the island, when life was just fun and games to him, seems like part of a "brighter childhood". But "thinking" does not come easily to Ralph; he keeps getting lost in vague thoughts, is distracted by unintentionally ambiguous phrases that come to his mind (such as "chasing imaginary ... [ghosts!]"), and tries again ... One thing, however, is clear to him: this assembly ahead of him must not be "fun", but well-ordered "business". Ralph has come to realize that the exclusive exploitation of "fun" has shown too obviously negative results. He is learning what it means to be chief, to conduct a well-organized meeting, to "go step by step", think logically, and arrive at a decision quickly when needed.
In his grim mood Ralph suddenly discovers "dirt and decay" around him; he notices the dirty state of his torn clothes; his long, tangled hair, and he becomes aware of how much he dislikes all this. His newly acquired insight makes him see the triangle of their assemblies as symbolically "irregular and sketchy" and he contemplates the boys' lack of reason with regard to the "ill-balanced twister".
Ralph's new mood of comprehension and speculation also leads him to a readjustment of his values. Now that he is forced to think, to be "wise", he realizes, and admits to himself Piggy's cleverness and brains. Unlike before, when Ralph was often irked by the fat, clumsy boy's "assmar", his "dull matter-of-fact ideas", and his laziness (cf. p. 70, l. 23!), he can now recognize "thought in another", Piggy's ability to think.

*The Assembly (Vb)*

The assembly, which begins rather late in the afternoon is, at first, marked by an air of special solemnity. Ralph is concentrating on a speech that he has planned point by point (cf. p. 88, l.4). Purposefully he repeats the sentences he considers important, dropping words „like heavy round stones" (!) in his attempt to "put things straight". He wants the boys to realize that rescue and survival depend on the observance of their social duties.
Ralph lists his queries systematically, in increasing order of importance, and argues them emphatically one by one: the neglected fresh water supply; the unfinished shelters; the toilet problem ("this place is getting dirty"); and, finally, the signal fire that is vital for rescue and is more essential than hunting pigs. Against their muttering of dissent, Ralph shouts his warning at the hunters to change their priorities. His announcement that there should be no fire except on the mountain top is followed by turmoil: a symptom of order beginning to crumble. But Ralph adamantly insists on their accepting his chieftainship ("Now you do what I say."), and repeats the points he has made with determination.
However, the most difficult step remains to be taken for Ralph as he attempts to sum up what has been worrying him most: "Things are breaking up. I don't understand why. We began well; we were happy. And then –" Ralph finds it hard to continue; but he is determined to discuss the fear that besets them, and find out what it is. Ralph freely admits that he himself is sometimes frightened, too, but

he can rationalize his fear and knows that it is nonsensical. He expects the boys to decide that their fear is unreasonable, and wants them to make a new start and to "be happy".

The sun is setting on the horizon as Jack begins to speak, denouncing the littluns as crybabies and telling them to put up with their fear "like the rest of us" – thus confessing to his own fear as well. But Jack only makes matters worse, spitefully scaring the littluns by mentioning "a dark thing", "some sort of animal", "a beast", yet at the same time denying its existence. By exploiting the children's fear of beasts Jack successfully undermines the effect Ralph's speech had on the boys.

When Jack says, despicably, "Be frightened, because you are like that", he seems to accept the fact that it is human nature to become fearful in the dark, but he also knows that fear, like bad dreams, can be lived with.

Darkness has set in by the time Jack has finished, and Piggy gets up to speak. Piggy's rational approach is meant to balance Jack's words and to support Ralph's speech. His realistic mind has an answer to every question. "If there's something wrong, there's someone to put it right." To Piggy life is "scientific". There is no beast, and there should not be any fear either. Or else they would be talking about ghosts next! (We remember Ralph's musings with regard to "chasing imaginary ... ghosts", before the meeting. cf. p. 88, l. 17) Piggy knows there is no need for fear, but then he hesitates and, revealingly, adds "unless we get frightened of people." Piggy is suggesting that fear may be caused by human beings themselves, not by some beast or other. Fear is a human product! (cf. also Piggy's significant comment that a "beast" would not eat pig. "*We* eat pig.")

But just as Ralph's speech was counteracted by Jack's words, Piggy's efforts are spoiled by two littluns, Phil and Percival, and by Maurice. Phil's vivid description of the nightmare he had, and of the horrid creature he saw moving in the trees, (Simon, on his way to his cabin as it turns out), and then Percival's hysterical crying and his whispering something about a beast that comes from the sea start wild arguing again. And when Maurice mentions the possibility of a giant squid coming out of the water this spreads further fear among the boys.

Ralph is watching this development in utter frustration. Until Percival started weeping and set off all the rest of the littluns crying in sympathy, the conch had been passed from speaker to speaker; Jack was the first to break the rule, cutting in and questioning Percival about the beast, but nobody minded ... Ralph is helpless, a "black, humped figure". His attempt at "getting things straight" has failed; instead he is witnessing "the breaking up of sanity". Instead of diminishing, the boys' fear keeps growing. Simon's attempt to explain the reason of their fear as being due to something inside the boys themselves ("... maybe it's only us") is contemptuously shouted down, as Piggy was before. It is too difficult for Simon to express "mankind's essential illness"; he tries to give expression to something bad and bestial deep inside man, something absolutely "dirty" that could be the reason for man's fear. But in the boys' "uncomprehending silence" that follows, Jack's insensitive, crude interjection ("Shit") beats Simon cruelly and renders him defenceless. Jack – like the others – does not understand Simon's intuitive explanation. Too late Ralph realizes that this assembly should have taken place in daylight; the darkness only creates more and more irrational fears, eventually even the suggestion of ghosts, something Piggy had tried to rule out when he spoke. Ludicrously enough Ralph clings to the democratic process of voting to decide whether ghosts exist or not. As if fear could be dispelled by a majority vote! The result of the vote renders Ralph speechless. Irrational convictions have completely usurped common sense and sober reason. Apparently most boys think there may be ghosts. This is too much for Piggy's rational mind. His vehement appeal turns into an accusation, promptly provoking an attack by Jack. Ralph's intervention results in Jack's openly turning against Ralph now, telling Ralph to shut up, showing his contempt of Ralph's concept of order; and consciously breaking the rules. "Who cares? – Bollocks to the rules!" At this point it is clear that Ralph's attempt at order has ended in complete turmoil and chaos. His rational approach has been counterfoiled by an irrational element present deep inside the boys. The assembly breaks up after Jack's announcement that they could hunt the beast if there was one. His wild excitement, the emphatic, rhythmic repetition "and beat and beat and beat!" presents just another way of coping with the boys' fear. It is an incantation against it! The same sort of incantation unites the boys again when they re-enact the pig-hunt and pig-killing in a revolving "black mass" chanting and dancing on the beach.

*After the Assembly (Vc)*

Ralph, Piggy and Simon are left behind in the deserted assembly triangle, "three blind mice" in the dark. Disgusted, they can hear the hysterical noises from the beach, where the boys have formed a circle and re-enact the pig-hunt. The primitive magic of the tribal circle contrasts strongly with the deserted 'parliamentary' triangle. The sound of the shell has been superseded by the sound of mock-hunting, chanting, "and real terror"!

Ralph and Piggy are miserable, helpless, and frustrated in the face of this situation. Ralph does not dare to blow the conch in case the boys should not follow the call and order would be destroyed forever. As long as the tribal incantation holds the boys spell-bound in their ritual, reasonable action and "daylight sanity" have no chance.

Much to Piggy's annoyance Ralph himself is beginning to have his doubts about the non-existence of ghosts or beasts on the island. Fear seems to be reaching out for him, too, now. When Ralph considers giving up his chieftainship, Piggy is horrified and, supported by Simon, implores Ralph to go on being chief. He knows the consequences Ralph's resignation would entail, and admits his deep-seated fear of Jack. Again, Piggy's analysis of someone being "frightened of people" is realistic and true (ll. 13–17); his remark "it's like asthma an' you can't breathe" is a clear-sighted comment: Piggy's asthma could be interpreted as an expression of his fear. He knows that Jack, as long as he can't hurt Ralph, would hurt "the next thing" – that is Piggy.

At the end of Chapter V fear reigns everywhere. Ralph's words are an apt summing up: "We're all drifting and things are going rotten." In their despairing mood Ralph and Piggy nostalgically recall the time when, at home, they could always turn to a grown-up for help, to Piggy's auntie, or Ralph's father ... However, Golding's bitter irony comes out clearly in the picture the boys have of "the majesty of adult life" (grown-ups having tea and discussing, not quarrelling ...); they forget that all the grown-ups' discussions did not manage to prevent the atomic war that is raging in Europe.

Ironically, Ralph is longing for a message, or a sign from the grown-up world, not knowing that such a "sign" is already on its way.

## Chapter VI: Beast from Air

*Sign from the World of Grown-Ups (VIa)*

This passage contains the immediate ironic response to Ralph's and Piggy's longing for "something grown-up ... a sign or something": the sign that comes down from the world of the grown-ups is a dead parachutist, shot down in a mighty air battle, just like the children were shot down in the passenger tube of their plane some weeks earlier. The war from which the boys were to be evacuated is still continuing.
The message of this scene is obvious: we are reminded that the "majesty of adult life" is a childish delusion.

"There is no essential difference between the island-world and the grown-up one. There too, order can be and has been overthrown; morality can be and has been inadequate to prevent wholesale destruction and savagery. The parachutist shows man's inhumanity to man, the record of what human beings have done to one another throughout human history. The children are revealing the same nature as the grown-ups, only perhaps more startlingly because of their age and their special situation. The child world is only a microcosm of the adult world." (Kinkead-Weekes, p. 38)

The dead man falls and crumples among the flowers, but cannot find his rest there, the wind catches his parachute and hauls him through the blue flowers until the lines get caught somewhere in red "shattered rocks". It is among the rocks of the mountain top that the figure comes to sit, "held by a complication of lines", seeming to bow and then lift his head again according to the pull exercised by the wind. The dead form is thus given animation.
He seems to peer "across the brow of the mountain", i.e. to the "unfriendly side" with the rocks and the open sea. Having come to rest on the mountain top he sits near the signal fire that the twins on duty have allowed to go out in the night.

*The "Beast" (VIb)*

The following scene vividly presents the twins, Sam and Eric, uneasy in the chilly darkness of the early morning, sleepy but managing to rekindle the signal fire.
Looking towards the rocks beyond the fire that is now burning brightly ("the wood exploding") and flinging a "circle of light" all around, the twins suddenly discover something that makes their blood curdle. Gripped in each other's arms, a picture of fear, they stare at a gap in the rocks near them; a gust of wind makes the forest "roar", sends the fire flailing and sparking, and causes a plopping noise from the thing they are staring at. Completely governed by fear they translate the dangling movements of the dead parachutist into a picture of a mysterious and horrifying creature. Terrified they flee to the beach below to wake Ralph and Piggy.
Ralph is woken from dreams that have mercifully removed him far from the island reality, dreams of "where he came from", a world of ponies, garden walls and "time for tea". This blissful dream of safety and comfort is relentlessly interrupted by the twins' exaggerated report of the "beast" they claim to have seen.
The twins' terror is catching: for Ralph and Piggy, too, the "maze of darkness" is "full of claws, full of the awful unknown and menace". Only after first light renders the situation a little more man-

ageable do they venture out of their shelter, but Ralph does not dare to blow the conch for the assembly that is now due to discuss "the dreadful news". Fearfully, the boys sneak to the platform. Apparently as an immediate consequence of the terrible news, the boys bring their spears to this assembly. Horrified, they listen to Sam and Eric's report, and almost instinctively form a fence of protection around them with their spears.

Chapter VI clearly demonstrates what Piggy and Simon felt before but did not know how to formulate: that fear is a product of the human imagination. Sam and Eric's own fear makes them exaggerate out of proportion what they saw in the rocks but did not recognize for what it was: a dead parachutist in a pitiful situation. They turn the dangling figure and the plopping fabric of his parachute into something horrible – a "beast" with wings, teeth and claws, a beast that they claim followed them, nearly touched them ... "Am I bleeding?"

Even Ralph and Piggy believe in the beast now; Ralph feels haunted, as if something kept watching them. Unlike Jack who is thrilled with the prospect of a "real" hunt and – without the conch in his hands to entitle him to speak – suggests going after the beast right away, Ralph feels that the beast cannot be hunted like a pig; wooden spears won't do against a mysterious creature that moves through trees and rocks, yet leaves no tracks.

Completely flustered, uneasy, Ralph is trying to think about meaningful action. He knows that they cannot just go after the beast without making provision for the littluns; his sense of responsibility tells him that someone has got to look after them. Typically, Jack's hunting instinct rules out any feeling of responsibility and compassion for the littluns. Jack couldn't care less. Just as before (p. 100, l. 16) he said "Bollocks to the rules! We're strong – we hunt!" so now he ignores care for the younger children.

Interrupting Piggy, Jack then openly challenges the authority of the conch and thus Ralph's leadership. There is a sudden crisis, an open struggle for power between Jack and Ralph, as the two stand face to face, Ralph flushed with anger, Jack white with the intensity of his feeling. "This is a hunter's job" stands against "Don't you want to be rescued?"; unbridled hunting passion against common sense. But the crisis passes. The need to re-light the signal fire, the boys' desire to be rescued brings them back on Ralph's side. As long as rescue is the boys' main objective, Ralph can assert himself. But Piggy's attack of asthma reveals how scared he is at this moment of tension. Eventually Ralph relents, and the boys decide to hunt the "beast" at the tail-end of the island where nobody has been yet and where "the thing" might live; a surprising decision, considering that the more likely place would be the mountain top where the twins saw the beast. Subconsciously perhaps the boys evade the uncanny, horror-ridden mountain top and rather move in the opposite direction first.

### *The Sleeping Leviathan (VIc)*

As Ralph, Jack, Simon and the biguns cautiously pick their way to the tail-end of the island their expedition parallels their first enthralled exploration of the island in Chapter I, and ironically contrasts with it. Things have changed with the advent of fear; a "beast" has established itself in the island paradise.

Simon is the only one not to believe in a mysterious beast; instead, the word conjures up in him a vision of "a human at once heroic and sick." Simon is thus intuitively aware of the answer to the boys' fear, but does not know how to convey the picture of "his inward sight" to the others. The dreadful "pressure of personality" makes him awkward and self-conscious; he expects the others to laugh at him, as indeed Ralph does when Simon does not mind where he is going and promptly bashes into a tree and hurts himself. Simon is a dreamer and, like Piggy, something of an outsider; but he does not suffer from a "personal hell" like Ralph, who is plucking up courage knowing that he will have to face a possible encounter with the beast at the "castle" rock. Simon's "I don't believe in the beast" are the last words that Ralph hears before setting out alone to explore the "castle".

The tail-end of the island lies almost detached (cf. p. 31, l. 13), cut off from it like a severed head, to be reached only over a narrow "neck", a rocky ledge over which the swell of the Pacific ocean sends foaming waves. The description of the "castle" with the "pink bastion" in front of it is forbidding; the way Ralph sees and experiences the narrow neck between the island and its headland assumes symbolic importance. For the first time Ralph understands that there are two completely different sides of the island: there is the "good" reef-protected side with the calm lagoon, the beach, the palm terrace, fruit-groves; and there is the "other side", the "unfriendly" side, the unprotected rocky shore with the swell of the open sea that to Ralph in his frightened state seems "like the breathing of some stupendous creature". Nature appears as threatening and demoniacal here; the sea is compared to a monstrous "sleeping leviathan". (Meaningfully enough, only Jack has been to this "other side" before.)

Contrary to what might be expected, Ralph's fear diminishes at the sight of this rough passage. He becomes cool and confident again, his common sense breaks through, and soberly he inspects the guano-covered rocks, finding "a sort of half-cave" with "rotten eggs" in it. The rotten birds' eggs and the white droppings all around on the barren rocks are suggestive of decay and dirt. In pronounced contrast to Jack who has followed Ralph and full of excitement senses the possibilities of a natural "fort", Ralph instinctively rejects the primitive wildness of this castle of rocks and considers it a "rotten place".

When Jack discovers boulders of rock that can be dislodged both boys remember their first exploration of the island, and the frolics and enthusiasm of their rock-rolling then. Perhaps we remember the description of that scene, too (p. 30): birds were fluttering up and white and pink dust was floating through the air as they sent a great rock smashing a deep hole into the forest 'like a bomb', or as if an 'enraged monster' had passed. A breath-taking if awe-inspiring game, played just for the fun of it. Now, however, there are sinister undertones in Jack's words as he suggests that "enemies" could be destroyed by rolling rocks down onto the narrow passage. While Jack is saying this, he and Ralph are looking down at the further end of the "neck" where the other boys are hiding in the grass, only their heads peering out. Exulting, in irrational aggression, Jack imagines a boulder's course of destruction towards them.

Counterpoising Jack's destructive energies, Ralph states the need to relight the signal fire on the mountain. However, once the other boys have realized that there is no beast and no danger they come swarming across and in no time start pushing a heavy rock into the sea in primitive childish enjoyment, completely forgetting the purpose of the expedition. It seems as if Ralph is now the only one to remember the signal fire. But when at the moment of his greatest anger he screams "Smoke" at the boys and petrifies them into silence, a "bat's wing" gives him a momentary blackout, as though Ralph himself had to force himself to remember that there is no time for fun and games now.

In any case Ralph cannot convince the boys any longer that rescue is the most important thing. Roger, for example, would clearly prefer to go on rolling stones, and others take up Jack's idea to have a "wizard" fort there. Instead of listening to the voice of reason the boys get carried away and imagine rolling rocks from the fort "right onto the bridge..." The attraction of primitive life is beginning to take over. At this point it seems that they would rather live in the caves of the rock than in the huts organized by Ralph on the palm terrace. The "game" of rock-rolling becomes a symbol of the gradual setting free of destructive forces, and foreshadows the later development.

Ralph has to put the whole weight of his authority against the mutinous boys to make them obey his order and make their way to the abandoned signal fire on the mountain top.

## Chapter VII: Shadows and Tall Trees

### *Depressing Island Conditions (VIIa)*

The more Ralph becomes disturbed by the boys' increasingly uncivilized behaviour, the more he becomes aware of their dirty outward appearance as well. On their way to the mountain Ralph has occasion to let his thoughts wander. Reflecting on his dirty state again (as he did before their third assembly, p. 83f.) he is so disgusted with his filthy appearance that he decides to do something about it. The fact that he has started biting his fingernails again, and his spontaneous utterance "Be sucking my thumb next..." are signs of Ralph's subconscious regression to early childhood habits which reveal his growing insecurity and helplessness. Applying "the memory of his sometime clean self" as a standard he then critically and "with a little fall of the heart" registers the dirty state of the other boys, and the conditions they consider "normal" now.

In his depressed mood Ralph turns his gaze away from the hunters who are doing their "business" just anywhere, making the island dirtier still, leaving their "droppings" like the pigs or the birds. But looking at the sea on this side of the island (the "other" side) with its endless rise and fall depresses Ralph further. When he first saw the open ocean (p. 115, l. 16) Ralph shuddered, it seemed like a giant monster to him; now, too, the sea appears wild and brutal as it breaks against the shore, the surf blown up from a gully (!) near him seems to reach out for him threateningly in "fingers of spray". The infinity, remoteness and indifference of the ocean makes Ralph feel "numbed", "helpless", "condemned", – lost.

However, Ralph's gloom is unexpectedly relieved by Simon who reads and understands the expression of despair on his face and comforts him in absolute confidence and conviction that Ralph will return to where he came from. Kneeling, and speaking down "from a higher rock" Simon is described like a prophet; even Ralph seems to sense the prophetic ring in Simon's words and is puzzled.

Meanwhile Jack is distracting the expedition again with his hunting urge, after he has found fresh, steaming pig's droppings. The excitement and dedication with which Jack bends over the excrements "as though he loved them" (!) is another marked contrast to Ralph's depression. As Ralph displays a growing concern about cleanliness and a civilized appearance, Jack is characterized more and more by the clay smeared on his face and his instinctive attraction towards droppings.

*Daydreams (VIIb)*

Ralph's day-dreaming is an escape from the disheartening reality around him. It takes him back to the cottage on the moors, to "Mummy" and "Daddy" and all the associations he has with "home", such as wild ponies, garden, snow flakes, a copper kettle, a bowl of cornflakes with sugar and cream ... Everything he remembers points at a comfortable British middle-class existence. Ralph indulges in his memories of the paradise of his early childhood, the real paradise, where "everything was all right" and "friendly". His day-dreaming is abruptly interrupted by the blunt reality of a "creature" rushing towards him with gleaming tusks and frightening grunts.

*Release of Violence (VIIc)*

Ralph's first participation in a pig hunt affects and drastically changes his mood, and reveals the fact that there is a darker side in him too. When his spear actually hits the boar's snout the same excitement flares up in him that besets the other hunters; "fright, apprehension, and pride" rule him, and he feels that "hunting was good after all"! His words "That was the beast, I think" show his pride at having courageously attacked the creature, but they also reveal a significant subconscious reaction: he has wounded living flesh and acquiesces in a feeling of guilt in his subconsciousness by suggesting it was the "beast" he hurt. Typically, Jack's sober comment brings him down to earth again.

Jack's reaction to Ralph's having joined the hunters shows his jealousy; his leadership as a hunter seems momentarily challenged. However, this time the hidden tension does not break out openly but is channelled in a different direction when the boys act out a mock hunt, with Robert miming a pig and everybody jabbing at him, including Ralph.

As on similar occasions before (cf. p. 81 and p. 100!) the game soon gets out of hand and becomes dangerous, "mock terror" turns into "real pain". As though Robert's screaming was only spurring them on further, the boys hit and hurt their victim; Jack "brandishing his knife" in savage fashion, Roger behind him. The accompanying ecstatic ritual chant urges them on even more, and Ralph too gets carried away by "a sudden thick excitement" and an "over-mastering desire to squeeze and hurt"!

The game is a game no more; the border line between mock-hunt and a ritual release of aggressions and violence has been crossed; the excitement of inflicting pain has been felt. Robert is almost killed in the boys' frenzied attack. After the climax, when they regain control of themselves, Jack rolls over, panting; to him it "was a good game". Ralph's uneasiness shows the return of his self-awareness, but Maurice's remark about the need of a drum and a fire points the direction the boys will go. They need a "real" pig "because you've got to kill him"; the game requires a victim if it is to end in complete satisfaction.

Jack's comment "Use a littlun" should not be taken seriously, but even this kind of joke is characteristic of the boys' degenerating moral standards and loss of conscience. It becomes increasingly hard to draw a line between "fun and games" and the display of darker, inchoate passions.

*The Search for the Beast (VIId)*

Finding his sense of duty again, Ralph urges the boys to be on their way to the mountain, after they have temporarily forgotten the beast over their "game". In spite of the twins' and Maurice's fear of the approaching darkness Jack insists on everyone going, and heads the expedition. As long as Ralph lets Jack lead the way there is no friction between the two boys, and Ralph can daydream again. But the boys' journey over the rocks along the "blinding" sea proves extremely hazardous; Ralph's feet are (really and symbolically) "less skilful than before", there is constant danger of slipping and falling down the sheer cliffs.

With darkness drawing nearer Ralph remembers his responsibility towards Piggy and the littluns. His noting that it is already "after tea-time" shows that Ralph is still conditioned by the social habits of the world he comes from. Again he finds thinking difficult (as before, cf. p. 85). Disregarding Jack's cynical interjection, Ralph accepts Simon's fearless offer to go through the forest all by himself and give Piggy a message.

When Ralph takes the lead over from Jack to find the pig-run that goes up to the mountain, the tone of Jack's voice immediately becomes offensive and vicious. It is obvious that he has started hating Ralph because he wants the leadership for himself. "Sensing the rising antagonism" Ralph tries to control himself but is provoked further by Jack. Any responsible action on this expedition is made impossible as Jack turns every decision that Ralph makes into a personal duel. Despairingly, but without really expecting an answer, Ralph asks Jack: "Why do you hate me?" He may be remembering what Piggy said to him (p. 102, l. 17ff.) "... you're chief an' he isn't."

This antagonism is bound to develop further. Not much later, after sunset, there is a "fresh rub of (the) two spirits" when Jack insinuates that Ralph is frightened, and "viciously" volunteers to go up the mountain alone if Ralph would not join him. Against his better judgment, against all reason, just to save face, Ralph goes with Jack. His seeming nonchalance is, in actual fact, a personal defeat.

The following scene is steeped in blackness. Ralph and Jack, unexpectedly joined by Roger, set out to climb the mountain in utter darkness. If their eyes were blinded by the sea in the late afternoon, they are now blinded by the darkness, and additionally with tears caused by the ashes of the burnt part of the forest that they have reached, and that should remind them of the boys' lack of consideration when (in Chapter II) their fire raged out of control. As though Ralph's common sense was reawakened by the recognition of those "small devils of dust", he risks another "rub" with Jack saying that they are fools going along in total darkness, and promptly becomes the target of Jack's mockery. This underlines the fact that their blindness is not just a physical phenomenon but a spiritual one as well. Both boys provoke each other with the accusation of cowardice until Jack ventures up to the mountain top alone, leaving Ralph and Roger behind in the dark, waiting.

*The Discovery of the Ape-like Creature (VIIe)*

The nerve-racking wait comes to an abrupt end with Jack's breathless head-over-heels return. After darkness and blindness have been stressed so much, Jack's horrified report that he "saw a thing" on the top seems sheer irony, the more so as just at that moment he blunders against the rocking trunk in the dark. But clearly Jack believes in what he "saw" – something "bulging" and "plopping" and, like the twins, he thinks the thing might be following him!

This time it is Ralph who feels bound to demonstrate a bit of "bravado", suggesting the three of them should "go and look"; and it is he who turns the situation into a personal challenge this time, overruling his "inner voice of reason", disregarding his foolishness, just yielding to "a kind of dentist's chair unreality" fostered by the darkness.

His attitude is just as unreasonable as Jack's was, and it does not come as a surprise that Ralph undergoes the same experience as his rival. The unlooked-for contact when his hands feel the ashes of the dead signal fire triggers off "green lights of nausea", the ashes blown into his face blind him again, his nausea grows. The extreme tension of the scene reaches its climax when Ralph, almost paralysed with nervous strain and with his teeth chattering, makes out a hump in the dark, and plucking up all his courage, takes two leaden steps forward. At this crucial moment Ralph's imagination is stimulated further by a roaring gust of wind and in the "confusion in the darkness" the dead parachutist appears to him (as he did to the twins and to Jack) as a horrible "creature", "something like a great ape", that seems to lift its head, presenting its decomposing "ruin of a face". With his nerves keyed up to breaking-point Ralph's fear now turns into terror, and taking giant strides, as Jack did before, he flees downhill in thoughtless confusion. He does not even realize that the "other creatures crying out" are Jack and Roger.

If the signal fire on the mountain top was originally representative of hope, reason and intelligence, the dead parachutist who has replaced it, could be seen as the deterioration of hope. Man as agent and victim of destruction in a war is ultimately reduced to a sub-human condition, and becomes an "ape" (!)- like creature. Without knowing it the boys are following the same course. They started their island existence with high hopes and great expectations, but increasingly abandon reasonable and intelligent behaviour in favour of instinctive, primitive existence. The more they give in to the pleasures of hunting, chanting, dancing, killing, the more their own image becomes like that of the "ape"-like man whom they interpret as the "beast".

## Chapter VIII: Gift for the Darkness

*Jack's Unsuccessful Revolution (VIIIa)*

It is a "dark mountain" that hovers above the boys on the beach at the beginning of Chapter VIII. Where the signal fire once represented a light of hope there is now the lair of the beast and the nest of fear. After their nauseating nightly experience Ralph, too, testifies to the existence of the beast now and, as the twins did, shudders as he speaks of its teeth and dreadful eyes. Piggy, doubtful and frightened at the same time, cleans the one lens of his broken specs, as though this might help him to see more clearly. But the boys' sight is impaired; the light of reason has been quenched by the darkness of their fear. Piggy's restless question "What are we going to do?" reflects the boys' helplessness in the face of a situation with no apparent way out.

The "thing" by the fire has taken the place of the signal, "as though it didn't want us to be rescued." Ralph is not aware of the fact that his way of looking at the beast is just a projection of his fear. But he knows that no signal fire means the boys are "beaten".

The conch, once so precious in its pearly purity, is no more than a "white blob" in the darkness now; its symbolic importance as a democratic tool is dwindling. And yet Jack suddenly reaches out for it to call an assembly, with the intention of challenging Ralph's position as chief. Jack's "legal" attempt to overthrow Ralph's leadership is triggered off by Ralph's realistic assessment of the hunters as "boys armed with sticks". It is the first time that Jack blows the conch, and he does it "inexpertly"! "Inexpertly" delivered are the points of his speech too. He demagogically misquotes Ralph and twists the facts to get his points across that Ralph "isn't a proper chief"; that he is no hunter, a "coward", and – a somewhat surprising regression into schoolboy mentality – "no prefect".

Jack has no sound logical arguments for his revolt; obviously he has no other reason for his rebellion but his own anarchic desire for leadership. When Jack tries to usurp control over the boys it is not to carry on Ralph's considerate, responsible, "democratic" guidance, but it is to assert his own power. However, for all his "tones of deep meaning and menace" Jack harvests nothing but embarrassed silence; none of the boys supports his motion, and his open rebellion comes to no avail. Repeating his menacing "all right, then", he lays the conch down in the grass in front of him; a most symbolically expressive gesture. This, and his decision not to "play" any longer suggests that he will no longer follow the democratic rules that the conch represents. Also, there is an unintentional ambiguity in his use of the word "play": from now on there won't be any more fair play, but relentless, harsh action. At the same time Jack's outburst "I'm not going to play any longer", once again has a downright childish ring, and his tears of shame and humiliation are those of a frustrated little boy.

Jack leaves the parliamentary triangle never to return to it, and disappears over the white sand into the darkness of the forest. The orderly grouping of the platform triangle will soon be replaced by the revolving movement of the tribal circle.

### *Desertions (VIIIb)*

Jack's desertion has a varied effect on the assembly. The boy who is most definitely relieved is Piggy, who thinks that without Jack they can "really decide on what's what." With Jack out of his way Piggy's opinion will count more now, and his brains can be recognized more clearly. Although he is still doubtful about the beast, he is playing it safe and suggests they should all stay near the platform, away from danger.

Ralph, however, is more depressed than ever before. Jack's denial of the rules and his revolt add to the burden he feels weighing on him, and his "Nothing to be done" sounds downright pessimistic.

Not altogether surprisingly, the only boy not to be scared of the beast is Simon, the outsider; but his timidly voiced courageous suggestion that the boys should climb the mountain (and see what the nature of the "thing" was) is contemptuously rejected.

Piggy's pragmatic proposal (ironically interpreted by Golding as "intellectual daring") to have a fire on the beach instead of on the mountain top brings a momentary relief from the boys' downcast mood. Clearly they want the fire not only for rescue but as a reassurance against the darkness. Preparing, lighting and maintaining the fire is a hectic distraction for the children (cf. similar episodes before) until Ralph and Piggy realize that a great many biguns have abandoned their responsibility and have secretly stolen away; they "won't play either" and have joined Jack.

Ralph falls silent at the recognition of this fact. His grim silence seems to remove him from the others and underlines his gloom and depression. Ralph's frustration comes out in his recently acquired habit of biting his finger-nails (cf. p. 120, l. 21!) Gratefully Ralph acknowledges Piggy's and the twins' well-meant efforts to cheer him up by surprising him with a load of fruit and inviting him to a "feast".

The validity of Piggy's "wise", self-satisfied comment "It's them that have no common sense that make trouble on this island" could be questioned. Is it really correct to blame only Jack and his hunters for things breaking up?

Meanwhile Simon has wandered off to the solitude and wild beauty of his jungle cabin. As Simon kneels down and a ray of sunlight falls onto him, the picture becomes highly suggestive of prayer and worship, and is slightly reminiscent of the portrayal of a hermit in his cell. It is as though Simon had something of a saint about him. The delicate beauty of the butterflies dancing in the air underlines the harmony and peace of this natural scene.

However, some inexplicable threat makes itself felt in the tremendous heat that is building up and making Simon increasingly restless and thirsty.

*Bloodlust (VIIIc)*

In a significant movement away from the platform and the conch Jack and the other deserters have met on the beach at the far end of the island, near the castle rock where they will eventually move to be able to barricade themselves in. Jack is "brilliantly happy" with his uniformed obedient hunters around him, who at one time, "ages ago" (in actual fact only weeks ago), were demure, angelic choir boys, but now constitute a tribal group controlled by their self-appointed chief. The decline of the boys' civilization is reflected in their outward appearance.

Jack's assertive, dictatorial "I'm going to be chief" allows for no communal discussion or democratic voting. There won't be any conch, or platform meetings with him. His only concern is "hunting"; no longer merely as a matter of getting meat, but as an unrestrained surrender to his savage instincts of tracking and killing.

Jack's offhanded suggestion that they should simply "forget" the beast and have no more bad dreams is sugared with his promise to kill another pig and have a "feast". What that feast might be like is easily imaginable; the contrast with Ralph's and Piggy's "feast" of fruits springs to mind immediately. Jack's feast is to lure even more of the biguns "away from the conch and all that". What Jack nonchalantly and vaguely sums up as "... all that" stands of course for common sense, civilized behaviour, awareness of responsibilities, rescue measures. Jack does not think of a signal fire, any thought of rescue is obliterated from his mind. More than ever Jack is associated with black shadows (p. 148, l. 1) and darkness; he is characterized as wearing "the damp darkness of the forest like his old clothes"! He has completely adapted himself to the dark side of the natural world. The ensuing pig-hunt in the oppressive afternoon heat is remarkable because of the increasing brutality of the kill and the almost orgiastic climax of the blood-steeped scene.

The way the boys go after the mother-sow, excited, almost intoxicated by the blood, "wedded to her in lust", and, as she falls, hurling themselves over the frantic sow in "dreadful eruption" – the whole scene is presented in a terminology that denotes strong sexual undertones. The ecstatic prodding, stabbing, pushing, and the "terrified squeal" that becomes a "high-pitched scream" are suggestive of a rape. The climax is reached when Jack, on top of the sow, "stabbing downward with his knife" cuts the animal's throat and feels the hot blood ejecting over his hands; finally the boys lie "heavy and fulfilled" over the collapsed sow.

The way Jack proudly shows the others his hands steaming with blood reveals how used he is to the sight and smell of blood now. His rubbing blood over Maurice's cheeks unwittingly imitates the blooding ceremonies of primitive societies. Jack has no qualms about cutting through the mother sow's belly; in expert fashion he takes the intestines out (p. 150, l. 12); and with remarkable stamina he cuts the sow's head off. Throughout this passage we note the realistic description of repulsive detail, an indication of how hardened some of the boys have become. Roger, impressed by Jack's superior handling of affairs instinctively addresses him as "Chief" now – a salutation never used for Ralph.

Roger is never far from Jack; he has played a prominent part in the killing too; in fact his is the only name besides Jack's to be mentioned. Not satisfied with killing the sow in true hunter fashion, Roger gets a sinister pleasure from actually torturing the pig by "leaning his whole weight" against the spear and driving it "right up her ass"! After having deserted the world of Ralph and Piggy, Jack and Roger now reveal what they understand by "hunting": following their instinctive violence, which is heightened into a thirst for blood as now there are no more moral restraints. It is Roger who sharpens a stick at both ends for Jack to jam the pig's head on, as a "gift" for the beast; Roger rams the stick into a crack in the rock and Jack fixes the dripping head – a pagan act of sacrificial offering to appease the beast. Buzzing flies over the guts have taken the place of butterflies! The "dim-eyed", "grinning" pig's head is so uncanny that it scares the boys and sends them running off as though it was the beast itself, another instance of the fact that the boys themselves create the object of their fear.

### *The Lord of the Flies (VIIId)*

From his quiet sanctuary Simon has watched the whole macabre act of the killing of the sow, the gutting and decapitation, and also the sacrificial offering. When finally the hunters run away from the object of their self-created fear, Simon stays on. However he keeps his eyes shut at first, not daring to look at the "obscene thing", the grinning pig's head whose eyes Simon feels are "dim with the infinite cynicism of adult life", a phrase strongly contrasting to Simon's, Piggy's and Ralph's earlier illusion of the "majesty of adult life" (p. 103, l. 7) and to be remembered towards the end of the book.

In the oppressive heat and the strange light before the tropical storm, with copper coloured clouds towering up, and flies buzzing where the butterflies were dancing before, Simon projects his own thinking into the pig's head. The voice he hears comes from within himself. It tempts him to take the easy way out, to run after the others, to take it all as "a joke", as a mistake. It suggests that perhaps a headache has made him imagine things and hallucinate.

Still keeping his eyes shut or at least sheltering them from the view of the grinning, blood-dripping sow's head, Simon experiences the "pearly stillness" around him as "illusive and without definition". As long as Simon does not dare to face the pig's head he is in the grip of the temptation to remain in illusion, and to avoid a clear "definition" of the reality of evil he has witnessed. This avoidance however, would make him partake in it. As if to demonstrate this fact, the horribly repulsive "black blob of flies" buzzes over from the pile of the sow's guts to find Simon and alight on him; after "gorging" themselves on the pig's intestines they now quench their thirst from Simon's sweat!

It is at this point that Simon raises his head and looks at what is now called the "Lord of the Flies" for the first time; and the grinning pig's head on the stick holds his gaze in a moment of "inescapable recognition" – an enigmatic phrase that leaves it to the reader to fathom its implications. Evidently Simon sees in the Lord of the Flies the reason for man's instinct towards evil and destruction.

The term "Lord of the Flies" or "Lord of the Dung" is a translation of the Hebrew word "Beelzebub" (a Philistine deity in the Old Testament), which is another name for Satan. It denotes something filthy, execrable, abominable, and we recall Simon's desperate attempt to express "the dirtiest thing there is" (p. 97). The boys' increasing filthiness, the deterioration of their outward appearance, their general loss of cleanliness and lack of personal hygiene, their being "taken short" all over the place, all indicate the direction they are taking. Especially Jack's going after the pigs' droppings, his sniffing of the fresh dung, but also his spilling of the intestines, the guts, the blood of the slaughtered animal associates him with the Lord of the Flies.

### *The Raid (VIIIe)*

Golding interrupts the scene of Simon's crucial encounter with the Lord of the Flies with the illuminating episode of Jack's raid on the fire, a demonstration of the boys' further regression to savage behaviour.

Ralph's depression is heightened by the prospect of the approaching storm, the strange light in the sky, the first bolts of thunder exploding "like a gun". Piggy is doing most of the thinking now, "like a grown-up" and Ralph, helpless and sighing, recognizes Piggy's rationality and turns to him for advice. The tables are turned now, as Ralph openly admits his fear to Piggy. What scares him most is not so much the beast as the fact that nobody (except Piggy) understands the necessity of having a fire any more, i.e. the importance of rescue. "Can't they see?" Ralph knows that the boys have reached a point where they just don't care any longer, and he senses the danger in himself that he, too, might not care one day.

Ralph is worried because his sense of responsibility is beginning to weaken. Both he and Piggy are "deeply troubled". "Unburdening himself" to Piggy, Ralph puts the tragic question to which he knows no answer: "What's wrong?" "What makes things break up like they do?" (cf. p. 89) As before, Piggy blames everything on Jack in a projection of his own deep-

seated fear, thus creating his own "beast". Note that Jack's name (... "him") has become a taboo for Piggy and Ralph, like the beast (the "thing"). A taboo implies the banning of something because some kind of fear has developed around it.
At that moment, as if a cue had been given, they are ambushed and their fire is raided by three howling "demoniac" figures, Jack, Maurice and Robert, who are painted almost out of recognition and look like savages (demons), more barbaric than ever before. Jack, naked except for a belt and the mask provided by the paint, invites the remaining boys to join his "tribe". "Me and my hunters ... We hunt and feast and have fun." This is the reduction to a formula that represents Jack's approach to island existence (cf. p. 41 Ralph: "We want to have fun. And we want to be rescued.") "Safe from shame or self-consciousness behind the mask of his paint" (cf. p. 69) Jack can look around him with compelling gaze, terrifying the littluns and making Piggy grab the conch in readiness to defend it. However, the conch does not interest Jack, it has lost its symbolic value for him. He just wants the fire, and to give a demonstration of his now established power. To mark the end of their appearance, the two "anonymous savages" by Jack's side are forced into a salutory chorus, "The Chief has spoken." – more atavistic ritual. Golding's vocabulary (tribe, demoniac, savages, etc) underscores Jack's boys' increasing regression to primitivism.
The boys' reaction to the savage raid is revealing: Sam and Eric first thought the savages were the beast – another typical projection of their fear. Piggy's fright has almost brought on his asthma; and Ralph suddenly feels the need for ritual. Ralph's reaction against the choric incantation of the savages instinctively leads him back to the platform and the conch, the outward framework of order and rational discussion, now more like a feeble bastion against savage and irrational behaviour. However, this meeting (the sixth in the book) threatens to slip through Ralph's fingers; he is flustered, stumbles at the word "fun" and nearly forgets "the most important thing", but Piggy's presence reminds him. Ralph sounds "lame" as if he was trying to convince himself as much as the others about the fire and rescue. It seems as though Ralph is beginning to doubt if reasonable behaviour is really all that important. He even admits that he too would like to put war-paint on and be a savage – demonstrating that the tendency to destructiveness is in him, too. The boys are hooked on their lust for "fun"; probably Bill voices everybody's opinion when he says "being savages ... must be jolly good fun". That and the prospect of meat plus possibly the threat of the thunder "booming like a cannon" eventually determines them to go to Jack's feast. Their constant yearning for fun and feasting predicts further dissolution, the destructive element is in all of them.
After this revealing interruption Golding continues the scene of Simon's encounter with the Lord of the Flies.

### *Simon's Confrontation with the Lord of the Flies (VIIIf)*

Simon's encounter with the Lord of the Flies is his moment of recognition of the nature of evil. The fact that he faces the gaze, not averting his eyes, not giving in to the temptation to run after the others and "forget the whole thing", enables him to see the Lord of the Flies for what it is: just a pig's head on a stick. Simon cannot be tempted to project his fear into the pig's head and consider it the "Beast". Even though the heat makes him a bit delirious and he feels one of his fits coming on (which may be why he imagines that the Lord of the Flies is speaking to him, whereas obviously the dialogue comes from within Simon himself) he knows that the pig's head is just an object that Jack has provided to compensate for his fear. He also knows it is wrong to believe, as Jack does, that the "Beast" is something one could hunt and kill, or propitiate. The "Beast", evil, is something inherent in human beings. "You knew, didn't you? I'm part of you."

The pig's head does not symbolize an evil outside the boys, but stands for the evil inside every single one of them, including Simon. This is what Simon must have known intuitively before (p. 97, l. 22) when trying to "express mankind's essential illness" he ventured to say "... maybe it's only us." The reason why it's "no go", why things are what they are, why things are "breaking up", why civilization fails, (and the answer to Ralph's question "what's wrong?") is that man is inherently evil.

In spite of his coming fit (possibly epileptic, considering Simon's shaking and his "arched and stiff" body) and his hallucination (the pig's head seems to "hang in space" and to expand like a balloon, the pig's mouth appears "vast" to him and grows in "blackness") Simon's inner voice reveals the truth he has realized in this encounter with the Lord of the Flies. Simon knows that "Beelzebub", the Devil, is the evil of unreasonable and irresponsible behaviour rooted inside them. "Golding seems to be saying that it does not matter what name you give to evil, call it devil, sin, neurosis, hate, violence, brutality; the important fact is that evil exists inside man and is a necessary part of the human condition." (F. Jackson, p. 26, cf. Bibl.) That is the implication also of the head's threat "You'll only meet me down there..." on the beach where the others are.

Simon is warned not to think that he could change the nature of the boys: "... do you think you know better than I do?" Simon's fearless recognition of the truth is not wanted. "Don't try it on ..., or else..." Simon's inner voice warns him not to interfere with the development of things on the island, and foretells his end if he does. "We shall do you. See?" "We" – that is "Jack and Roger and Maurice and Robert and Bill and Piggy and Ralph" – all of them.

The Lord of the Flies insists "We are going to have fun on this island!", echoing Jack's words (p. 155, l. 7) but also Ralph's, when the boys first explored the island (p. 41, l. 3) and the word "fun" had a different ring; the reader is made aware of how significantly the boys' original idea of fun and games has changed. "Fun", unrestrained surrender to primitive, savage, atavistic passions is the maxim of the Lord of the Flies, as it is representative of the urge within the boys.

When Simon loses consciousness at the end of this encounter he faints into his own new awareness of the nature of evil.

## Chapter IX: A View to a Death

### *Simon's Good News (IXa)*

When Simon comes to again the air is still charged with the threat of the approaching storm, but Simon – although weakened by his fit – is feeling better now. After going through his purgatorial confrontation with the LoF Simon feels freer, and after a period of rest he has completely lost any fear of the LoF hanging on its stick "like a black ball". The black and fluorescent green flies that make the split guts look like "glistening coal" don't impress him any more and significantly enough they leave him alone now. They "explode" with a vicious note just as the atmosphere is "ready to explode" when Simon starts moving among the creepers. Simon knows clearly what to do now. Loud, with conviction and determination, he repeats the words he whispered to the others on their fifth meeting (p. 142, l. 15) "What else is there to do?" Simon has known all along that there is only one thing to be done to cope with the cause of the boys' fear: to go up to the mountain and find out about the "thing".

On his way to the mountain top Simon almost effortlessly lifts the entangling "ropes of creepers" aside and thus symbolically tackles and removes the impediments that have so frequently obstructed the boys' progress. Simon's slow climb up the mountain is, of course, charged with symbolism; the mountain top stands for clearsightedness and the recognition of truth. When Simon makes his way up to the top a "pearly light from the sky" falls onto him, singling him out, embellishing him with brightness. On the other hand Simon is described as proceeding almost like a sleepwalker, "drearily", with an empty face, wearily, and yet knowing the direction he is meant to go. He moves without excitement, yet without any fear either; the "usual brightness (has) gone from his eyes", and he walks "like an old man". His encounter with the LoF seems to have made him older, and wiser; with the awareness of the nature of evil Simon has become seeing and determined.

On discovering the horrid "humped thing" on the top Simon is not scared off by the roaring wind which uncannily accompanies his approach (as the other boys were, cf. p. 107 and p. 136!), nor by the dark cloud of flies around the decaying creature's head, but he looks and "sees". Going down on his knees he involuntarily assumes a kneeling position (cf. p. 146, l. 24), but then moves on, sees clearly, understands the "mechanics of this parody", examines and understands the details, and eventually disentangles and "frees" the dead parachutist. He can free the poor, dangling body that the other boys' fearful imagination had turned into a "beast", because he is himself free now. The encounter with the rotting parachutist complements that with the rotting pig's head. Simon's experience here completes his knowledge of what the nature of evil is that afflicts the boys.

Simon's vomiting, brought about by the terrible sight and foul smell of the decaying corpse, is a perfectly understandable release, and at the same time can be interpreted as a purgation from his fear and from his encounter with the LoF, and an expression of his catharsis, a purgation of the horror of realization.

From now on the "beast" is beast no more for Simon. He has recognized the truth that the beast is in fact harmless (if horrible). There is no reason for fear or superstition. Looking down from the top of the mountain at the boys on the farther end of the beach Simon is filled with only one thought: the good news must reach them as soon as possible. At this moment Simon is like a prophet on the mountain who goes down to spread "the good news" (cf. p. 109, when the twins spread "the dreadful news").

### *Ralph and Piggy's Isolation (IXb)*

Meanwhile, coping with the oppressive heat under the "looming sky" by swimming in their pool, Ralph and Piggy reveal their irritability by almost having a row. After Piggy has calmed down again and the two boys notice that they have now been almost completely deserted by the other boys, they find it hard to hide their uneasiness and to pretend that they don't care. Piggy's suggestion that they ought perhaps to go after the others, too, shows his sense of loss and isolation; his hastily added "to make sure nothing happens" is clearly revealed as a flimsy excuse by the fact that he blushes.

*The Storm / Simon's Death (IXc)*

Jack's lot (note the derogative term for 'group' now used) has moved towards the farther, wilder part of the beach where there are hardly any palm trees, and "white blown sand" fringes a rock. Jack himself is seated on a log as Ralph used to be when he was presiding over the group as chief (cf. p. 84). But Jack sits on the log as though it were a "throne"; more than that: painted and garlanded as he is, he sits there "like an idol", awe-inspiring. Although depicted with subtle irony the image of Jack sitting raised, in powerful silence, provided with drinks and piles of meat and fruit, has a disconcerting effect on Ralph and Piggy, as is revealed by their silly giggling, which only poorly disguises their uneasiness.

A kind of "normality" is restored only after Piggy is once again turned into "the centre of social derision", which ironically enough allows Ralph the opportunity to mix with the others again. At this point in the course of events, laughing at the expense of the underdog seems to be the only common basis left for some sort of communication between Jack and his lot, and Ralph; – another revelation of the sinister side of human nature.

It is interesting to note how Jack is described now, self-confident in his "pride of ownership", impatient, threatening, as he scrutinizes Ralph and Piggy from behind his paint, and speaks in an imperative manner. He has a littlun to wait on him as a servant, and although there appears to be a good deal of irony in the bombastic "Power lay in the brown swell of his forearms; authority sat on his shoulder and chattered in his ear like an ape", there is yet the terrible aura of the usurper about him, and the word "ape" with its implied distortion of the human image, assumes a deeper meaning. Ralph's realization that evening has come "with the threat of violence" refers to the approaching thunderstorm as well as to Jack's imperious and threatening behaviour.

Jack's claim to leadership is obvious. The majority of the boys obediently follow his domineering, imperative order to sit down, and after his thrice repeated (and thrice delayed) summons "Who'll join my tribe?" willingly subscribe to their new leader, whose appeal to their pleasure-loving side ("have fun"/"tribe") contrasts distinctly with the sense of responsibility Ralph had displayed at earlier meetings. Ralph's various attempts to interfere prove futile; the conch "doesn't count at this end of the island", a call for an assembly will not be heard and answered! Ralph, "confused", helpless, gets no response to his appealing words from the ranks of boys; the idea of rules and order, and of rescue, has become meaningless to them.

When at this moment the storm breaks and heavy raindrops beat down on the unsheltered boys, Jack intuitively reacts by inciting the boys to do their dance, thus counteracting a possible diminishing of his authority, and providing a protective ritual to distract the boys from the frightening turmoil of the thunderstorm.

The ritual circle brings the boys close to each other and constitutes a "demented but partly secure society" that limits the boys' terror to a certain degree – including

Ralph's and Piggy's – and makes it "governable". The ritual enacts the "hemming in" of the boys' own terrors which they project into the "beast". However, the magic impulse of the regular chant and of the steady rhythm of the tribal dance, the ecstatic dedication to the imitation hunt, and the mounting hysteria caused by the flashes of lightning and the crashing of the thunder, so affects the boys that superficial excitement develops into the release of some fearful power that is building up in the hunters. The imitation pig-hunt has inadvertently become a beast-hunt: it is the object of their fear that the boys are pretending to kill. "Kill the pig" has turned into "Kill the beast"; and scared as they are in this tropical thunderstorm, the words of their chant channel the boys' ecstasy into a strong, blind desire for a victim, a scapegoat for the beast.

At this point of extreme, almost unbearable tension the boys' terror has reached a peak also and needs an outlet; and when a scared littlun blunders into their ring that momentarily "yawns emptily", he is immediately jumped at and attacked ("Him! Him!"). Unwittingly the boys act out Jack's frivolous suggestion in response to Roger's comment "You want a real pig, because you've got to kill him", when he said "Use a littlun" (p. 127, l. 13).

The littlun has a narrow escape, however, as at the peak of intensity the boys are suddenly distracted by a dark "thing" that comes crawling out of the forest: Simon, exhausted from the day's experiences and from his long strenuous walk, is trying to tell the boys the truth about the "beast" on the mountain. The fury of the storm's incessant lightning and thunder, but even more the demented, orgiastic chanting and dancing, drown Simon's words; and in tragic irony he himself is blindly attacked by the mob of boys who – conditioned to expect a "beast" outside themselves – have found their scapegoat at last. Miming becomes reality. They "do him in", (p. 168, l. 20, cf. p. 159, l. 10). The picture of Simon kneeling (once again!) in the centre of the murderous circle (which is vividly described as a crunching "mouth"), folding his arms over his face, stands out as a focus on human suffering and sacrifice. Simon, the only one not to be blinded by self-inflicted fears, the boy who is not scared of darkness and who comes like the prophet from the mountain to bring the "good news", is not listened to, is not even recognized by the crowd of terror-stricken and "beast"-ridden boys, and is driven to fall over the steep edge of the rock. At this point when in delirious ecstasy they strike, bite and tear Simon to death, the boys have turned into anonymous, primitive savages (cf. the wordless "tearing of teeth and claws"!). Obliviously performing their "beast"-killing they have turned into wild beasts themselves, surrendering completely to primeval instincts at the total expense of reason – a first macabre climax in the development of the novel.

With Simon imagination and religious knowledge are quenched. As Simon understands the nature of evil on the island he is a threat to the continuance of that evil – and is therefore killed. All the boys participate in this killing, which points to the universality of their guilt. They needed a scapegoat for the presence of evil on the island and, tragically, hit on the least appropriate target.

When the cleansing torrent of water drenches and sobers the boys they realize, at last, how small a "beast" it is that has become the victim of their frenzy. No mention is made whether or not the boys recognize whom they have killed.

Significantly, as Simon is lying lifeless on the beach, the dead parachutist on the mountain top (who had been freed by

Simon) is moved by a sudden gust of wind, falls towards the beach and is then carried out to sea.
Spiritual darkness prevails as the boys rush screaming "into the darkness".

*Simon's Disappearance (IXd)*

By strong contrast with the ecstatic and tempestuous violence of the preceding holocaust, the final passage of Chapter IX is filled with the refreshing peace and quiet after the storm. The maddening, oppressive heat is over now, the midnight air is cool, moist and clear.
So far in the novel darkness and blackness have nearly always been associated with dangerous and destructive qualities; significantly enough the clouds drift away now and the reign of darkness is overcome by the "incredible lamps of the stars" that shed their light on the refreshed earth and on Simon's maimed body that has been left behind after the orgy and lies "huddled" and bleeding on the beach.
The whole passage is steeped in the imagery of light, brightness, and clearness. There are at least seventeen references to light (clear, bright, silvery, fiery, phosphorescence, etc.)
There is something mysterious, almost mystic, in the description of Simon's departure. "Moonbeam-bodied creatures with fiery eyes" attend to him in the "advancing clearness" and make a "patch of light" around Simon's blood stains; Simon's hair is "dressed with brightness" like a halo; his body is "lifted" and is gently and softly moved out towards the open sea, where water and sky blend. A host of highly suggestive phrases mysteriously associate Simon's poor broken body with Christian notions of crucifixion and resurrection.

## Chapter X: The Shell and the Glasses

*Shameful Burden (Xa)*

"After what had happened" Ralph and Piggy climb the deserted platform with "befouled bodies", the betraying signs of the nightly orgy still on them, and sit in leaden silence. The worn grass in the triangle underlines the sense of emptiness and loss: there are to be no more parliamentary assemblies, as all the boys except for the twins and some littluns have deserted Ralph and joined Jack's tribe.
With an effort, clearing his throat, then whispering, Ralph gives expression to the shameful, terrible burden on his mind: "Simon". His bad conscience, embarrassment, and shocked emotions reveal themselves when Ralph kneels down, takes hold of the conch and caresses it, as though trying to conjure up the spirit of order it once represented. Ralph's desperate question "What are we going to do?" rings with the same tragic quality as it did in Chapter VIII (cf. p. 153f.). Piggy's feeble attempt to suggest calling an assembly falls flat before Ralph's sharp laughter of despair. At this point, and in the passage that follows, Ralph is more rational and clearsighted than Piggy. Piggy would be only too glad to see things differently from what they are on this morning. Ralph, however, is facing reality. Shivering, and against Piggy's shrill protest Ralph puts into words what he has come to realize: the killing of Simon was "murder". Piggy, who cannot even get the word 'murder' over his lips, is making excuses, trying to rationalize the events of the night, blaming them on the thunderstorm, on their being scared. But Ralph does not accept these excuses. Whilst he had always relied on Piggy's advice

before, Ralph for the first time applies his own judgement here and gains his own insight.
He knows that much more was involved than being scared; it was something else that made him participate in the killling. Piggy's search for a "formula" proves futile; Ralph cannot be consoled with any of Piggy's eager suggestions ("He may still be alive"; "... only pretending –"), and his "low and stricken" voice stops Piggy short. Holding the conch in his arms as though it could comfort him, Ralph laments the "things we did". His "we" implies a confession to his part in the killing; the loathing in his voice betrays his revulsion at the horror of the bloody orgy, yet at the same time there is a "feverish excitement" in his voice, even now, at remembering the dance. It is the same "sudden, thick excitement" that carried him away in the mock hunt (p. 126!). Ralph senses, and is afraid of, the darker side in him that causes this sensation. He is frightened – "Of us." Like Simon when he suggested the beast might be "... only us" (p. 97) Ralph has taken a step towards the realization of his own human, fallible nature, of "mankind's essential illness." He does not close his eyes to the fact that all of them participated in the fatal dance ("But we were! All of us!"), and accepts responsibility. Ralph's "baffled common sense" (p. 77) and his longing for decency and the lost paradise finds expression in his "Oh God, I want to go home."
Piggy, however, stubbornly refuses to "see". He claims it was "an accident", best forgotten quickly. Besides, he says, they were only on the outside of the circle, i.e. not directly responsible for what happened. By denying their involvement in Simon's death, Piggy shows his unwillingness to accept their guilt. "We never done nothing, we never seen nothing"!
Sam and Eric, too, are filled with shame and a bad conscience as their "flushing", embarrassed greeting, and evasive chatting show, but they, like Piggy, claim their innocence ("we left early") washing their hands of it, although their outward appearance betrays them.
However, the air is "heavy with unspoken knowledge", and all four boys are shaken by the memory of the "dance" that they claim not to have participated in!

### *The Fort (Xb)*

The reaction of Jack's lot to the horrors of the dance that led to Simon's death is remarkably different from Ralph's, Piggy's and the twins'. Unlike Ralph, who confesses to his individual responsibility, "each savage flinched away from his individual memory" (p. 177).
Following Roger on his way back to Jack's tribe, we realize that Jack has moved his group to the very end of the island now, to the rock mentioned early in the book (p. 31) "almost detached, standing like a fort ... with one bold, pink bastion" the opportunities of which Jack immediately recognized when the boys were exploring that part of the island: "What a place for a fort!" (p. 116) Now this rock with its half-cave, rotten eggs and guano (cf. p. 116) has become "Castle Rock" (the capital letters indicating that Jack has given a name to the main bastion of his realm) and to Roger's mind this is "the safest place" to hold out against the horrors of the island!
The neck of land leading towards Castle Rock is guarded, the cliff is fortified, and more ritual is employed (Roger is "challenged" by a sentry, and Jack has become "the Chief" – obliterating his name just as the paint blocks out his face!). Typically, Roger is highly impressed by the ingenuity with which a log has been placed to lever a huge rock down onto the

neck if required, and admires Jack as a "proper Chief".

Roger's loose tooth and his glancing "sombrely" back at the island are hints at his part in the nightly feast; and Robert changes "the unspoken subject" (of Simon's death!) to speak about their Chief and his authority. The "feast" and the killing of Simon was a release of all the dark forces within the boys and has meant an end of everything the conch represented. Irresponsible behaviour has triumphed; there is nothing left now but absolute power, which Jack wields over his tribe. He has a boy tied up for hours and beats him for no apparent reason! But to Roger's mind the "possibilities of irresponsible authority" appear as an "illumination"! Rocks, cave, tribe, Chief, savages – the terminology that seems so naturally to describe the situation shows the enormous development the schoolboys have undergone since their arrival on the island. Jack's choirboys are "savages" now, and not just pretending. Their games have become reality.

In ritual obedience to their Chief they improve the cave (while Ralph's shelters by the platform disintegrate!) and prepare to "defend the gate" against "the others"; Jack manages to establish a vague image of an enemy, which by a stroke of intuition he cleverly connects with the "beast", harping on the boys' fear, and referring to Simon's death: "... remember how *he* crawled –" By suggesting that the beast came "disguised" he confirms the boys' belief that killing Simon was the only thing to do. There is no need then to hide what they have done, as long as they are convinced that the "beast" is something outside them that can appear in different shapes and be killed in those shapes. This is made clear when one little savage (obediently putting his hand up as in school!) asks "But didn't we – (kill the beast last night)?" Jack's answer suggests that the "beast" couldn't ever be killed, but might be propitiated if the boys "keep on the right side of him"! This speculation on the "beast" is diametrically opposed to Simon's realization that the "beast" is not something external to man, but is inside him!

The fear of the beast that Jack has fostered in his tribe is counteracted by his promise of a feast (just as their dance is to serve as a protective measure "if he comes".) The fire for the feast must be stolen from Ralph and Piggy.

### *The Theft of the Glasses (Xc)*

The beginning and the end of the last part of Chapter X focuses on Piggy's glasses; it deals with vision and blindness, in more than one sense.

Piggy's glasses mean sight for him and fire for the others. The fire itself has in the meantime taken on the double function of providing smoke signals and being a comforting hearth, the latter becoming increasingly more important, a safeguard against the threatening darkness at night, although the four boys find the fire too hard to keep up, the more so as the wood is damp.

The implication of Eric's disheartened question as to what good it is to keep a fire going shocks Ralph, as he realizes that he himself must labour to remember what Piggy had once called "the most important thing" – rescue. There is that black curtain flapping in his head (cf. p. 180, l. 28) that keeps interfering with his hope "to get out of this mess."

Resigned, and "defenceless" in the beginning darkness, Ralph leads the few boys left on his side to the remnants of their battered shelters.

With darkness come uneasiness, fear, nightmares ...

Ralph's groaning in his sleep is echoed by the twins' "dreadful moaning", disturbing Piggy and keeping him awake. The maddening "blanket-thick" darkness fosters the boys' fear; the "beast" becomes a reality for Ralph and Piggy when uncanny noises suggest the presence of a "thing . . . prowling" outside; Piggy's convulsive grip and his attack of asthma reveal his terror. Once again the boys' own fear projects a "beast" external to them; and once again a frenzied, unthinking, reckless, anonymous release of animal emotions – "hitting, biting, scratching" – follows in the dark. The parallel with the attack on Simon is obvious; as long as the boys are blinded by their fear they fight with "passionate hysteria", getting satisfaction from the release of their brutal aggressiveness no matter who is hit. Although Jack is identified by his "vicious snarling", the intensity of the blind fighting does not allow for any discrimination; the only thing that counts is the grim enjoyment of inflicting pain and feeling a face becoming "slippery" with blood. (Afterwards it dawns on them that Ralph in his fury has hit Eric and Eric retaliated on Ralph!)
The collapse of the shelter signals the climax of the destructive animalism of the fighting; it also signals the ultimate collapse of civilization on the island.
The purpose of Jack's raid on the shelter was not, as Piggy fears at first, to steal the conch, but to steal Piggy's glasses. The conch has no meaning for Jack and his savages any longer. The stealing of Piggy's (already broken!) glasses, however, – revealing an almost sadistic lack of concern for Piggy who will be nearly blind without his specs – gives to Jack the means of fire and thus completes his absolute power. When Jack raided Ralph's fire before (p. 154) he just stole half-burnt branches, now he has got the lens. Ralph and his friends are left with hardly any means of survival, and Jack's demonstration of the possibilities of irresponsible authority promises worse to come.
The theft of Piggy's glasses might be interpreted as the defeat of the intellectual by the savage. Henceforth, Piggy's clearsightedness and his "brains" will be severely curtailed.

## Chapter XI: Castle Rock

### *The Seventh Meeting (XIa)*

Blindness prevails as Ralph, Piggy and the twins are sitting helpless in the cold morning air: Piggy is practically blind without his glasses, Ralph with one eye closed by the swelling and the other blinded with the ashes of the dead fire, and Erik looking through a mask of dried blood. Almost pathetically Piggy and Ralph cling to their democratic rules as symbolized by the conch and the assembly that they call just for themselves and a few littluns to discuss their predicament.
Once again the sound of the shell sends birds crying "as on that morning ages ago"; however, the situation has now changed completely. Flustered and confused, with Piggy's helplessness adding to his difficulties, Ralph is "trying to think". In a confused, associative manner rather than in logical sequence Ralph attributes the blame for the boys' degression into savagery entirely to Jack, unwittingly projecting properties to his scapegoat that he himself shares. Ralph's question, "Are we savages or what?" is, of course, rhetorical, implying that they are not; and his naive attempt to turn the wheel backwards by washing and brushing themselves "looking like we used to" becomes deeply ironical if we remember that

Ralph's words "– after all we aren't savages really ..." echo exactly what Jack said at their second assembly (p. 47).
In spite of the release of inner darkness in Ralph on the occasions of the killing of the sow, the killing of Simon, and the night fight in the shelter, Ralph is unwilling to accept that he is a "savage" too; unlike Simon, he has not penetrated to that level of self-awareness. The "black curtain" that flaps repeatedly in his brain is an indication of Ralph's partially blinded insight.
Piggy, too, is blind in more than one respect. He has always displayed a fervent faith in the conch, and has been the one who most strictly enforced the right to speak as long as a boy held the conch. The same fervour comes through now when Piggy wants to carry the conch to Jack and show him "the one thing he hasn't got." But he overestimates the symbolic value of the conch completely; to Jack it has become meaningless. In his trembling determination to go to "that Jack Merridew" and tell him, Piggy gains almost tragic stature. He is going to demand his glasses back "because what's right is right". Piggy relies on a moral imperative: Jack has "got to" give his specs back. However, Piggy's claim is based on the old concept of order which is not valid any longer. There is only the "shape of the old assembly trodden in the grass" to listen to him, and "Jack Merridew" has become an anonymous "Chief".
Worked up as he is, Piggy disregards Ralph's warning, and also Sam's. Ralph's words "You'll get hurt" contrast with the words Simon spoke to Ralph (p. 122) "You'll get back", a phrase Ralph suddenly remembers now and which makes him decide that they should go with Piggy.

*Expedition to Castle Rock / The Crisis (XIb)*

Ralph's, Piggy's and the twins' expedition to Castle Rock takes an ominous route: first they go along a part of the beach that is compared to a cleaned blade, suggestive of a freshly sharpened executioner's sword; then they pass the place of their "dance" where Simon was killed; and they skirt the "densest tangle of the island" when they eventually reach the narrow "neck" of land that leads to the severed head of Castle Rock.
There is a heightened sense of danger when Ralph guides the frightened Piggy onto the neck, and forty feet below them the sucking sea reveals a table of granite, reminiscent of Ralph's first crossing over, when he shuddered to see the swell of the waters "like the breathing of some stupendous creature", like a "sleeping leviathan" (p. 115). The sudden "war-cries", the sentry's challenge, Roger's gloomy, dead-serious face add further tension. Roger is now doing himself what he experienced before (p. 175), and his "You mind out – see?" contains a terrible threat. Ralph's long sounding of the conch, and his twice repeated call for an assembly is received with a snigger, as if Ralph was suggesting something ludicrous.
Even before Jack appears from the forest Roger cannot resist the dark impulse in him to throw stones at the twins from his height, startling Sam so much that he nearly stumbles over the edge. It is the same impulse that he first displayed when throwing stones at little Henry (p. 67), some evil power in him that begins "to pulse" and to take possession of him – related to the impulse that makes Jack go after pigs and kill them.
Jack on his return from a routine pig killing (a sow again!) is masked in stark

"black and green", a pronounced contrast to Ralph's longing for cleanliness! Ralph in his attempt to get Piggy's glasses back uses Piggy's terminology that Jack has "got to" return the specs, but Jack's arrogant reaction shows how ineffective Piggy's intended moral appeal is.

The clash of Ralph's temper and Jack's results in a mad fight, in which Jack aims the "lethal point" of his spear at Ralph's chest. Jack has got so used to hunting down and killing pigs that in his fierce, aggressive mood he now almost goes for Ralph's life as well. Ralph's second attempt to convince Jack that he has "got to" return Piggy's glasses refers to a code of honour from their schoolboy education, "You aren't playing the game", – only produces giggles from the tribe, which demonstrates how ridiculous the old rules and civilized values have become.

Neither Ralph's frustrated appeal nor his gust of rage can impress the "painted anonymity" of the savages. Laughter is their response to such words as "signal fire", or "rescue". The "painted fools" don't understand Ralph's concern any more. All they feel is the "otherness" of the intruders, and "the power in their own hands". They obey Jack's tyrannical authority, "grab", "fell", and "tie up" the twins (whose ludicrously civilized expressions of protest reveal the absurdity of good social manners under such conditions). In view of such blatant ruthlessness Ralph has to realize how ineffective, indeed ridiculous, his reliance on any sort of moral basis in Jack has been, and the crisis is imminent.

Ralph's screaming means both a release and a signal of attack. In his fury he uses a most revealing terminology when calling Jack a "beast", a "swine" and a "thief". To Ralph Jack stands for everything unreasonable, unsocial, irresponsible, evil on the island; Jack is the reason why things are "no go", he is indeed a "beast" in Ralph's eyes; and in his animal behaviour (cf. Jack's vicious snarling, his sniffing of the pigs' scent, and now his "grunting" when hit in the stomach) he is like one of the "swine" that he hunts.

### *Piggy's Death / The Destruction of the Conch (XIc)*

When Ralph's and Jack's ferocious fighting is unexpectedly interrupted by Piggy's courageous intervention (Piggy trusting the authority of the conch, but the tribe listening to him only momentarily as to a clown), Roger's ominous stone-throwing from his height further increases tension. From Roger's height – a hundred feet above the narrow causeway (cf. p. 116) – the boys hardly look human: Ralph is reduced to a "shock of hair", and Piggy "a bag of fat".

However, Piggy rises to great stature when he says what he feels he has got to say, telling Jack's boys off for acting "like a crowd of kids" (cf. Piggy doing the same thing in Chapter II, p. 42 and p. 50), and then – holding up the "magic shell" – shouting his two questions, which for all their simplicity are powerful rhetoric. Supporting Piggy, Ralph takes up the rhetorical pattern of juxtaposition that Piggy has started, and sums up the conflict that has determined their island existence from the start: "Which is better: law and rescue, or hunting and breaking things up?"

Piggy's and Ralph's joint effort is a last desperate attack of reason and common sense against the bastion of savagery and irresponsibility.

However, Jack's yelling and the screaming of his mob drown the voice of reason and Ralph can no longer make himself heard. A "solid mass of menace" is about to attack; and a "storm of sound", an "incantation of hatred" marks the second crisis in this chapter.

For a brief moment the situation seems frozen: on the neck of land Ralph and Piggy alone, practically defenceless, the latter holding out the conch, his fragile "talisman"; on the other side the whole painted tribe of savages "bristling with spears", ready to release their irrational hatred. At this moment of extreme tension Roger, overhead, yields to that source of power he feels pulsing in him and in "delirious abandonment" levers the "monstrous" rock down that kills Piggy and destroys the conch.

(The falling rock sparks off memories of the wonder of the boys' first exploration of the island, when Jack and Ralph in playful excitement send a big rock downhill smashing a scar through the forest – not realizing the implications of their game, although the description of the forest shaking "as with the passage of an enraged monster" (p. 30) contains a sense of dire foreboding.)

Piggy's death is described in realistic detail; he dies like a pig ("with no time for a grunt", his arms and legs "twitching like a pig's".) his nickname drastically borne out. Like Simon, Piggy falls to his death from a rock; for a moment he is lying on that square flat red rock in the sea that Ralph had seen "spread like a table" on their first excursion to the neck (p. 115) The "table" is like an altar on which Piggy lies sacrificed, before the sea, the "leviathan", "breathes" again (cf. p. 115; "like the breathing of some stupendous creature") and swallows Piggy up.

Significantly, Piggy's head is broken open, his brain is destroyed. Piggy's brains are not in demand with these savages; reason and intellect are obliterated. At the same time the conch explodes into fragments and "ceases to exist", another symbolic event, indicating the ultimate loss of democratic order and the right of speech so cherished by Piggy.

However, as A. Johnston notes, whereas Simon is described in language befitting a dead saint, Piggy is pictured as a dead animal.

"Of course, Piggy's actions immediately before his murder are brave in conventional terms; but his rationalist's faith in order and human perfectibility, ironically undercut throughout the book, seems nowhere more misguided than in this scene. The mystic's intuitive recognition that good and evil coexist within man is the spark of his divinity; but the rationalist's denial of such intangible forces chains him forever to the material world of earth and organism." (A. Johnston, p. 16)

Piggy's death stupefies Ralph, but kindles Jack and his mob to vicious violence. Jack endorses the murder of Piggy by stating "I meant that". The spears hurled at Ralph are aimed to hit, the one going past Ralph's face could have killed him. As the bloodthirsty savages with their "anonymous devils' faces" come swarming across the neck, the comparison with flies alighting on Ralph lends itself.

Panic-stricken and instinctively Ralph runs for his life. A witchlike noise "as of sea-gulls" rises behind him, reminding us of the eerie cries of birds that so often scared the boys, but this time they are the shrill, ecstatic war-cries of Jack's mob for whom there is no more restraint now. Ralph's jumping over the headless body of the sow that Jack has killed underlines the impression that Ralph himself is like a terrified chased pig.

### *Roger – the Torturer (XId)*

The attention at the end of Chapter XI is focused on Roger, who has come down from the heights of his pinnacle to be nearer the scene of action, "the hangman's horror" around him. We remember how in Chapter IV, restrained by the habits of a civilized upbringing, Roger cannot throw stones directly at a human being (p. 67); how he overcomes this restraint in the pig hunt in Chapter VIII, where his behaviour is wild, frenzied, and he leans "with his whole weight" on the spear which he pushes into the sow (p. 149); how he admires Robert leaning on the lever that "would send the rock thundering down to the neck of the land" (p. 176); how "some source of power" begins to "pulse in Roger's body" (p. 194) that, eventually, makes him lean "all his weight" on the lever (p. 200).

Roger, the furtive boy of the beginning "whom no one knew" (p. 23) has become the executioner. The way he now advances on Sam and Eric, ready to assist his Chief in torturing them, fills the twins with unspeakable terror. Recalling Roger "assimilating the possibilities of irresponsible authority" (p. 176) we now see him "as one wielding a nameless authority" himself. Liberated from all restraint and control Roger, the hangman, has become the torturer as well. He is just as merciless as Jack.

## Chapter XII: Cry of the Hunters

### *"Ambushing Fears of the Night" (XIIa)*

The island's metaphorical scar in the opening chapter which has been cut into the forest by the crashing plane, is now mirrored in the real, bloody scar over Ralph's ribs.

Hiding in the thicket like a wounded animal and listening with keyed up nerves for any noises of pursuit, Ralph peers at the boy on guard on the cliff top, Robert, whose tossing up of a pebble is an ominous reminder of Roger's throwing small stones before levering the monstrous rock. The "fatal knowledge" of the deaths of Simon and Piggy comes back to Ralph, and with it the conviction that these savages "would go further and further". Also, Ralph is aware of some "indefinable connection between himself and Jack" which has existed from the start when "baffled in love and hate" (p. 60) they recognize their different capabilities and standards. Ralph has something of Jack in him, and Jack will never be really free from Ralph and the standards that he represents until Ralph is dead.

Terrified at the consequences of his musings, Ralph attempts to escape his own logic by making himself believe that "they're not as bad as that" and that Piggy's death was "an accident"; just as Piggy did not want to acept the truth of Simon's murder at first and insisted it was "an accident". (p. 173)

In defiance of his better knowledge, Ralph decides to ignore the "leaden feeling about the heart", and once again to try and "rely on their common sense, their daylight sanity", – a pitiful, failure-doomed decision, dictated by his anticipation of the "ambushing fears of the deep night" (p. 205, l. 11) as he is sitting all alone on the deserted platform, shivering.

### *Ralph and the Lord of the Flies (XIIb)*

The clearing where Simon had his encounter with the Lord of the Flies lies somewhere in the middle between the now deserted platform and Castle Rock: the fulcrum between the seats of democratic order and anarchic freedom. It is there, where rock prevents vegetation from growing and the "slanting sticks" of sunlight can hardly penetrate, that Ralph, too, has his confrontation with the grinning Lord of the Flies.

The continued decay has turned the pig's head into a skull "gleaming as white as ever the conch had done", a reminder of the fact that whereas the fragile beauty of the conch has ceased to be, the deadly white skull with its "horrible grin" continues to exist. Like Simon, Ralph looks "steadily" at the Lord of the Flies; like Simon, he interprets its grinning as a "cynical jeer" (cf. p. 151, where Simon experiences the pig's half-shut eyes as "dim with the infinite cynicism of adult life"!); like Simon, Ralph has the impression that the skull may not be entirely lifeless. – However, the Lord of the Flies does not "speak" to Ralph as it did to Simon. To Ralph the skull seems "to know all the answers – and won't tell"!

Accordingly, Ralph's reaction is diametrically opposed to Simon's: his sick fear, loathing and rage is the opposite of Simon's response. Whilst Simon understood and accepted the message of the Lord of the Flies (cf. p. 162), Ralph's rage and hitting out can be interpreted as a rejection of that message. Ralph does not acknowledge his own nature, but fights the recognition of evil. He does not want to realize that the "filthy thing" will always "bob back" in the rhythm of man's darkness; that its grin will for ever remain – even if it is six feet across.

Ironically the "spear" that Ralph holds in defence between himself and the grin is the stick on which the Lord of the Flies had been lodged and on which it moved to and fro; this stick will accompany him henceforth, an extension of the evil he is backing away from. The skull remains behind "grinning at the sky": an image of evil forever mocking heaven, certain of its victory.

*Encounter in the Dark (XIIc)*

Hiding in the thicket, Ralph is torn between a hopeless longing for "daylight sanity" and the realization of "darkness and the horrors of death". His moaning shows his despair. If only he could, in schoolboy fashion, go up to the fort and ask for "pax". But the waves "breathing" on the unfriendly side of the ocean are a warning reminder to Ralph of Piggy's death.

Ralph's tragic situation is emphasized by the exquisite line "He knelt among the shadows and felt his isolation bitterly." The whole paradox of Ralph's outcast state comes out in his words "Cos I had some sense." Because he had displayed a sense of communal duty, of concern for the group and their rescue, a sense of responsibility, he has been deserted by the others to whom "fun and games" seem more tempting; although he always tried, with the best intentions, to do what made sense, he is now hunted like a beast.

The discovery that Samneric have been brainwashed and have joined the tribe, destroys Ralph's last secret hopes. He is now left in utter isolation. Crawling up to the twins "as though he were blind" (cf. Piggy!), constantly aware of the breathing leviathan ocean and the death rock below him (and with the stick that supported the Lord of the Flies as a weapon in his hand) Ralph scares Sam and Eric into horrified stuttering. (For a moment they seem to think Piggy's ghost has appeared from the death rock.)

It is depressing to see how easily the twins have succumbed to the tribal habits. Eric jabs his spear in the air like the savages now and uses their vocabulary ("shove off", "they'll do you"). Ralph feels a "dull pain" about "these things", especially when questioned about their own determination in the hunt the twins squirm: their fear of being tortured again by Roger is so deep-seated that if it came to the worst they would probably betray Ralph.

Ralph's question "What have I done?" is merely rhetorical and Eric's response revealing: "Never mind what's sense. That's gone." Jack and Roger are going to hunt and kill Ralph like a pig; and the twins are going to participate in the hunt. Significantly, Ralph's question "What are they going to do?" becomes a comprising "What are *you* going to do when you catch me?" Although Ralph does not comprehend the stupendous implications of the answer "Roger sharpened a stick at both ends", the reader does. We remember the scene when Jack cut off the pig's head telling Roger to sharpen a stick at both ends (p. 150) so that he could jam the head onto the "pointed end of the stick" (p. 151).

Five times in this passage the "flowering" death rock below Ralph is mentioned "where Piggy had fallen". The memory of Piggy is with Ralph permanently; like the twins he is haunted with the idea that Piggy could rise from the water "with his empty head" and blind. Thus, the fact is corroborated again that "sense" and reason are irrevocably gone; Ralph is left with nothing but his "horrors of the supernatural" and his fear of the savages, the latter being heightened by the renewed torture of one of the twins.

### *The Holocaust (XIId)*

When Ralph wakes up from "age-long nightmares of falling and death" (a phrase that shows how deeply the memory of Piggy's fatal forty-foot fall is seated in his subconsciousness), the ululations he hears "like the cry of a flying bird", the repeated cries of the hunters eager to track him down, sound like a distant echo of the first "witch-like cry" heard on the island (p. 7) and also of the hoarse, echoed cries after the discovery of the "beast" (p. 108).

For a while Ralph has the illusion of safety, hiding in the free space smashed into the thicket by the bouncing rock that killed Piggy. However, his hideout is soon revealed when under torture the twins betray Ralph, bearing out what their ominous silence foretold the night before.

The monstrosity of the situation is underlined by the savages' "silvery laughter" that is so entirely out of keeping with the twins' gasping and squealing. This "silvery", unreal, eerie laughter has been heard before (p. 197) infuriating Ralph with its paradox display of ignorance and total disregard of moral values.

The repeated "high bird-like cries" and someone's cynical laugh tell Ralph that the hunt is still on; his extreme nervosity is revealed in his gnawing the spear now (instead of his fingernails, cf. pp. 120, 145), as he realizes that Jack is trying to kill him by rolling rocks over the top of the cliff. The rocks smash scars through the thicket and jolt the earth just as the big rock that killed Piggy did (p. 200). While Piggy, however, was killed in "delirious abandonment", Ralph is purposefully hunted down with almost military strategy. The biggest rock on the cliff, as big as "a tank" (!), is sent down on Ralph, turning over "slowly as a millwheel" (cf. p. 117, 26), and flinging Ralph through the air without actually hitting him.

The animal in Ralph comes out now that he is governed by his instinct of self-preservation. Panic-stricken, he wards off the attack of a savage by thrusting his own spear into him. With his spear raised and "snarling" like an animal driven into a corner Ralph himself is now ready to draw blood in self-defence. He knows that he is in for worse to come when a savage utters a shocked "No!" Again, the irrationality of the savages' excited laughter adds an element of uncanny ruthlessness.

Realizing that the forest has been set on fire to smoke him out, Ralph becomes savage himself; "snarling", stabbing, he hurls himself at one of the hunters, then races along the pig-run "like a boar", driven on by the shrill cry of the hunters, dashing on with no time to think, "no Piggy to talk sense", and the "dignity of the conch" a thing of the past.

Ralph knows that he has heard the "deep grumbling noise" of the burning forest before, i.e. when due to Jack's boys' negligence the mountain top on "the unfriendly side" was ablaze (p. 48ff.), "the noises of the fire merged into a drum-roll" (p. 49) and the fire "growled" at them (p. 50). At that time the boys were shocked to see their rescue fire rage out of control. But they did not learn from their mistakes. On the contrary, this time they have set the forest on fire quite deliberately, regardless of the consequences, and "the drum-roll heralds an execution quite literally." (Kinkead-Weekes, p. 62).

When in heedless fright, chased by the cordon of the battue, Ralph stumbles by the "fathom-wide grin of the skull" in the clearing again, the LoF's jeering grin is no longer mocking the blue of heaven, but is answered by black blankets of hellish smoke, as the savages' blind frenzy has set the whole island on fire.

Fugitive Ralph trying to retreat into "the darkest hole on the island" finds a matted jungle cabin very similar to Simon's hole (cf. p. 61) where he listens to the "drum-roll" of the fire.

The "volleying shots" of bursting trees are reminders of those threatening explosions of the first fire (p. 51); and the flames eating up the fruit trees recall Piggy's words "Won't we look funny if the whole island burns up? Cooked fruit, that's what we'll have to eat, and roast pork. And that's nothing to laugh at!" (p. 50) Ralph's fleeting thought "– what would they eat tomorrow?" reflects a last instance of reasonable thinking, an echo of Piggy.

From the moment of Ralph's recognition that the stick he wrenched from the rocky crack (p. 205/206) is sharpened at both ends, and the realization of the implications of this for himself, the strain on him becomes almost unbearable. The stick in his hands becomes a vibrating "stake". At the point of greatest tension when Ralph looks an ambushing anonymous savage straight in the eye, prepared for a vicious attack, he suddenly remembers Simon's words "You'll get back", a prophecy that seems ludicrously wrong and mistaken in the face of this hopeless situation. At this point Ralph's frenzy comes to a peak and needs a release. His scream of "fright and anger and desperation" marks Ralph's flight. With the howling mob of the savages behind him like a "fringe of menace" Ralph becomes an epitome of hopeless fear. The last thing he registers before he falls and is down on his knees in the sand, is a shelter bursting into flames – a last instance of the total collapse of civilization on the island. Then, fallen Ralph "with arms up to ward off" the fatal blow, cries for mercy.

If the book had ended here the reader's imagination would have brought the scene to its most likely conclusion ...

### *The "Rescue" (XIIe)*

Golding ends his book with an unexpected dramatic device, when the moment of Ralph's imminent death is turned into the moment of his rescue. The climax of the action is at the same time its turning point. Ironically, the smoke that signals the destruction of the island has attracted a British warship, and the savage hunt is stopped.

There is a drastic change of perspectives at this point: Ralph "down" in the sand, staggers to his feet and looks "up" at a neatly uniformed naval officer; the officer, in turn, looks "down" at the filthy boy in front of him. The appearance of the British officer suddenly reduces the howling "savages" to "little boys" with "sharp sticks" in their hands "making no noise at all" now.

Surprisingly, the officer reacts with no more than cautious, ironical astonishment, taking the situation entirely at its face value. The "kids" look like "scarecrows" to him; they need a good nose-wipe, a bath, ointment – that's all. The officer's comments show a complete lack of insight into the situation; he speaks of "fun and games" (unwittingly echoing one of the crucial phrases in the book, cf. pp. 155, 159, 166, etc) while the flames are devouring the last palm trees on the platform and the sky is black with smoke! His question "Having a war or something?" is accompanied by a cheerful grin. Little does he know of the primitive "war" the hunters have been waging against Ralph, of the bloodcurdling, scaring "bird-like" cries those small "scarecrows" in front of him have uttered. He does not realize the ambiguity of his own metaphor when he sees their "distended bellies of small savages", nor does he understand Percival's loss of self-identification, or the meaning of one "little boy" starting forward in answer to the question who the boss was, or of the fact that this boy is wearing the "remains of an extraordinary black cap on his red hair" and is carrying the remains of a pair of glasses, like a scalp, at his waist. Not for a moment does it dawn on him that the boys have paralleled the eternal pattern of development of the adult world in creating their own holocaust.

Realizing the necessity for a tiresome search through the scorched island for any stray boys, the officer comes out with the typical cliché of "a pack of British boys" who ought to have "put up a better show than that", ironically revealing the same naive confidence as Jack does at the beginning ("We're English; and the English are best at everything" p. 47).

The officer is grossly mistaken when he speaks of a "jolly good show" and mentally compares the "pack" of boys to Ballantyne's heroes in 'The Coral Island'. His easy optimism significantly belies Piggy's trust that "grown-ups know things" (p. 103). The officer's cheerful grin reveals his callous ignorance, and is the author's cynical comment on "the majesty of adult life". His grin refers back to and connects him with the fathom-wide grin of the Lord of the Flies and its cynical jeering. It may be the same "amused" grin that Simon experienced in his encounter with the Lord of the Flies and compared to "the infinite cynicism of adult life" (p. 151).

Ralph's remembering for a brief moment the "glamour" that had "once" invested the beaches accentuates the distance the boys have covered since those first days and of which the officer knows nothing.

When Ralph eventually breaks down and in "shuddering spasms of grief" weeps for "the end of innocence, the darkness of man's heart, and the fall through the air of the true, wise friend called Piggy", we know that Ralph has grown into the sort of insight the officer turns away from. The child has gained knowledge of the "darkness of man's heart", the adult remains ignorant.

Thus the change of perspectives at the end of the book forces the reader to "measure the gap that separates what the officer sees from what we ourselves know." (Kinkead-Weekes, p. 63). Like Jack's savage hunters the officer is a symbol of the chain of destruction that exists both on the island and in the outside world. The uniform, the revolver, the cutter with the sub-machine gun, and the trim cruiser in the distance on which the officer's eyes finally rest ("a little embarrassed" by the children's weeping) are representative of the weapons of the adult, "civilized" world.

Thus the vicious circle is closed: the children who were to be saved from a Europe burning up in an atomic war, have turned their newly found paradise into scorched earth and are only accidentally saved from their burning island by a cruiser which (as Golding wrote to his publisher) "will presently be hunting its enemy in the same implacable way. And who will rescue the adult and his cruiser?"

*The Meaning of the End*

"The end of the book comes unexpectedly at a time when Ralph is doomed; it is like the waking out of a nightmare. Ralph is saved only because the adult world intervenes; yet his rescuer is on the point of returning to "adult" war, a nuclear war which is in numerical terms infinitely more extravagant in its potential disaster. Given the barbaric chaos the boys have been reduced to, the officer appears to them (to us) as order. It is only on reflection that the reader remembers that the officer is involved in a nuclear war and yet is still 'order'." (V. Tiger, p. 54)

Golding's own explanation supports this view: "The whole book is symbolic in nature except the rescue in the end where adult life appears, dignified and capable, but in reality enmeshed in the same evil as the symbolic life of the children on the island." (quoted in F. Jackson, p. 42)

The end of the book does not therefore offer any solution. It leaves open the question of how the development of the boys' society from idyll to nightmare, from order to chaos, might have been prevented.

Golding demonstrates that the "innocence" of children is a myth, that the powers of darkness are part of human nature and therefore to be found in children as well as in adults. The effect that civilization has on the boys, the "taboo of the old life" turns out to be only skin-deep when the boys are placed in a primitive situation. The gradual deterioration of the civilized element, which begins almost with the discarding of the boys' clothes, is reflected in the increasingly disrupted form of their meetings and also in their expeditions where the original rational purpose is constantly forgotten for the sake of irrational games, such as rolling rocks and smashing scars into the forest.

In their "innocent" games the boys reveal the same destructive drives that the grown-ups display in their large-scale war; the wounds the children smash into their island forest correspond to the 'scar' the crashing plane left behind, and ultimately to the waste land caused by an atom bomb.

When the little savages and the officer from the trim cruiser stand face to face at the end of the book, the wheel has come full circle. There is deep irony in the confrontation of the children's regression to a state of primitive savagery with the progressive, highly sophisticated equipment of the modern version of savagery: warfare.

*The Parable*

For all its clarity of outline, Golding's *LoF* is a very complex novel. What begins like just another island-adventure-survival book, soon turns into a parable of the development of fear, violence and brutality. Unlike Defoe's *Robinson Crusoe* or Ballantyne's *The Coral Island,* the boys' immediate problem is not so much survival (obviously the island provides them with everything that is vitally necessary). The real problem turns out to be the "snake-thing", the "beastie" – that is very soon blown out of proportion into a formidable "beast". Clearly the boys themselves create the object of their fear, and then succumb to it more and more, which is paralleled by their own degeneration into savagery, until the civilized schoolboys of the beginning have changed into the primitive cavemen of the end. "This indicates that the individual ... is unable on its own to free itself from the captivity of its own ignorance and fear and to overcome its inherent attachment to evil" (Jackson, p. 43). Obviously it is this selfsame inability to free itself from ignorance and fear that has, time and again, led mankind into wars and destruction.

It would seem that Golding was familiar with Thomas Hobbes' *Leviathan* (1651) when he wrote *LoF*, as the inevitability of the boys' movement toward savagery corresponds with Hobbes' philosophical thesis that the nature of man is the predicament of man.

"... in the first place I put for a general inclination of all mankind a perpetual and restless desire of power after power that ceases only in death. ... Competition of riches, honour, command or other power, inclines to enmity and war ..." (T. Hobbes, Leviathan, Part 1, Ch. 11, ed. by M. Oakeshott, Blackwell, Oxf., o. D., p. 64).

It seems no coincidence that Golding makes metaphorical use of the word 'leviathan' at the end of the first half of the book (p. 115) when the boys' regressive movement is gathering momentum; the "sleeping leviathan" conveys more than just a Biblical association with a monstrous whale (cf. Psalm 104:26), it implies the evil powers that lie dormant but ready to wake up at any moment.

The title *Lord of the Flies* seems to suggest a basically religious treatment of the theme; and the book is, indeed, concerned with Beelzebub, the devil, the incarnation of evil. However, an interpretation should not be limited to the theological explanation of how the serpent entered Paradise and caused the fall of man.

The theme (or themes) of Golding's story can be interpreted in a number of different ways, such as those listed by Weiand:

"Original sin, the fallen nature of man, good and evil in the human heart or in the group, the awful possibilities of man's free will, the necessity of the discovery of self as a safeguard against evil, the weakening of social and religious norms in a godless world, an allegory of individual, social and political regression, the loss of civilized restraints and taboos due to a lack of awareness of the awful penalties for disregarding them, the dangers inherent in heedless self-expression at the expense of communal obligations (duties), the awful consequences of unbridled hedonism as a major principle for the conduct of life ("ego-trip") in individual and community. The major theme is the destruction of the myth of the island and of childish innocence, an initiation into the awful possibilities of evil even in the hearts of mere children." (Weiand, p. 92/93)

Above all, though, *LoF* is a story of man's fall. The word "fall" can be taken quite literally as well as metaphorically. It is human violence and warfare that causes the boys to fall onto the island and to disturb its natural, paradisiac peace. It is for the same reason that the dead parachutist falls onto the mountain top.

When Simon is brutally knocked to pieces by the boys' blind frenzy he falls off a rock before he is killed by the crowd, and Piggy, of course, falls to his death when Roger hits him with a huge rock. These literal falls correspond to the boys' metaphorical fall from the state of innocent, civilized childhood behaviour at the beginning to the savagery of the end. Not only do the boys (like Adam and Eve) lose their initial paradise, but so total is their mad succumbence to the irrationality of evil that eventually they scorch the very ground they live on, in a hellish fire. This theme of the boys' "fall" is illustrated by a complex metaphorical structure that contributes to the overall effect, such as the boys' discarding their school uniforms and putting on masks of paint, the killing of pigs with increasing brutality, the throwing of stones and rolling of rocks, the growing filth and sloth, the breaking of Piggy's glasses, the breaking of the conch, the sacrificial gift of guts to the pig's head, the development of primitive ritual, etc.

The dimensions are extended further by the mention of white "stones that had lain on the sands of another shore", "token of preposterous time" and of "white wave-worn sticks" or of rocks that "soon, in a matter of centuries" would become islands (p. 115), adding a wider perspective in time and space, as if to point out that the forces at work here are of timeless validity.

"'LoF' suggests a large scale of human values, social, political, moral and mythic which are relevant in both universal and contemporary terms, but it isolates and roots these concerns in a boy's world, a world where real boys make a mess of things." (V. Tiger, p. 54)

*The "Message"*

What then is the message that Golding wants to put across? Is it to show how thin the veneer of "civilization" is? Is it the unmitigated recognition that even the innocence of childhood is a pathetic fallacy, that human nature is tragically defective and man's capacity for evil boundless? Is it the awareness that – given the outward circumstances – man will be driven by elemental, primitive forces? Is it an allegory on the rise of fascism or despotism in general? Golding himself wrote to his publishers: "The theme is an attempt to trace the defects of society back to the defects of human nature." But then he went on to say: "The moral is that the stages of a society must depend on the ethical nature of the individual ...".

This comment would seem to allow the possibility of a positive influence of human ethics on a society. We are made to remember Simon and Piggy, both outsiders and both victims, but representing the "ethical nature of the individual"; and of Ralph, too, who in spite of the "black curtain" that flickers dangerously in his brain, clings to the idea of responsible behaviour. In spite of the fact that *all* the boys (with the exception of Simon) are in constant danger of succumbing to their fear of the beast, Golding shows us – through Simon, Ralph and Piggy – the only way to escape from regression into the darkness of barbarism: by recognizing that evil (= the "beast") is a product of the human mind, generated by man himself. Thus Golding's book should be understood as a contribution to critical self-awareness, and as a warning against man's potential for brutality towards his fellow man.

Common sense and intelligence must be enhanced by firm moral principles if the course of humanity is not to take the direction outlined in Golding's book.

*The Technique*

Golding tells a straightforward story, tracing the progressive development of a chain of events in roughly chronological order with only a rare flashback or two. The apparent simplicity of the narration has led many critics to think that Golding's language is correspondingly simple. This, alas, is a fallacy. Only the schoolboy slang dialogues are "simple"; most of the descriptive passages however are written in an evocative style that is frequently burdened with unusual words and is sometimes unnecessarily ornate. Occasionally Golding even makes up his own words to gain a special effect (e.g.: p. 10 *flink,* p. 18 *wubber,* p. 27 *magicked)*

Of great importance is Golding's subtle yet persistent use of imagery and symbols. Perhaps the most meaningful image is that of the island boat (cf. p. 31) moving steadily backwards! The gradual regression of the boys' society towards Stone Age standards is thus foreshadowed early in the book. The island boat is reflected also in the assembly boat whose apex significantly points towards the darkness of the jungle (cf. p. 84) suggesting the course into darkness that the boys are steering.

The imagery of light and darkness, and the many shades in between (cf. for instance p. 35, or p. 85) is full of meaning, and so are the mirages. There is a whole network of related images. The book abounds in unobtrusive symbolism, some of which may go unnoticed unless the reader is sensitive enough to respond to the connotative meaning some words are charged with.

For example, there are fertile palm trees, but also parasitic creepers on the island; fruit trees, but also dead trunks; saplings, and skull-like coconuts; "snakes", birds with witch-like cries, flies, – and butterflies; there is the pig's head and the conch; the smell of droppings and dung, and the scent of "candle-bud flowers", there are sticks and stones and Jack's knife, but also Piggy's glasses; the caves and the shelters; the jungle and the mountain top; there are the two sides of the island; there are two types of fire; there are parliamentary triangles and tribal circles.

The same pattern of juxtaposition and complementation can be observed in the boys themselves: there are the biguns and the littluns; there is the multicoloured bunch of boys around Ralph and the black uniformity of the choir boys around Jack; there is Piggy, the rationalist, and Simon, the imaginative (or mystic); Jack, the compulsive hunter, and Ralph, the responsible organizer; there is Piggy to side with Ralph, and Roger to side with Jack. On a larger scale, the whole island society with its conch, meetings, expeditions, hunting and fighting finds its replica in the outside adult world of megaphones, officers and war.

Then there are unexplainable ambiguities. What, for instance, is the connection between the first "witch-like cry ... echoed by another", and the various other mentions of echoed birds' cries in later stages of the book, to the savages' echoed ululations "like the cry of a flying bird" (p. 211) at the end of the novel?

It is through their interconnection, through a pattern of repetition and contrast that the symbolic implications become increasingly clear in the course of the novel. Thus, for example, the assemblies develop from an ordered grouping into a "sketchy and irregular" triangle which eventually disintegrates completely into a mere deserted "shape" trodden in the grass.

Correspondingly, the demure, civilized schoolboys of the beginning undergo significant developments, as is mirrored in a great many details. Roger offers a good example to be traced through the book. The inconspicuous, furtive boy who first throws stones at little ones aiming to miss, and derives deep satisfaction from rolling rocks downhill, yields more and more to his desire to inflict pain and kill (cf. sow episode) until the teaser has become the torturer and executioner.

Another point worth noting is Golding's technique in handling the point of view from which he tells his story. While most of the book is told from the point of view of omniscient narrator, who observes the actions of the boys mainly from the outside, Golding achieves a special effect by sometimes entering the mind of a character and seeing and feeling through him, as it were. (A good example of this is provided in Chapter III, especially in the description of Simon.) This allows Golding to change from the author's to the child's perspective. The most abrupt change in perspective and point of view occurs at the end when Ralph is on his knees and the officer rescues him. The children's perspective is, of course, maintained throughout in the dialogues, which are imbued with typical British schoolboy slang. On the other hand, it is in passages such as p. 169/170, when he describes Simon's mysterious departure, that Golding is at his most detached, because he is also at his most artistic and "symbolic".

# Lesson Plans

## Chapters I to III: "We've got to have rules."

### Lesson 1: Introduction of the Topic / The Initial Situation

#### Didactic Considerations

A first approach to the theme of Golding's *Lord of the Flies* aims at motivating the students, at arousing their curiosity and interest. This could be achieved by beginning the course with a talk about some famous conventional island adventure-and-survival books that most students should be familiar with, such as D. Defoe's *Robinson Crusoe,* or R. L. Stevenson's *Treasure Island,* and a discussion both of the problems involved in such a desert island existence, and of the different emphasis the authors laid in their respective books. The teacher could acquaint the class with other novels that might be mentioned in this context, such as Ballantyne's *The Coral Island* (cf. p. 122), R. Macaulay's deeply ironical *Orphan Island* (where a shipload of English orphans are wrecked on a South Sea island and gradually turn the island into a replica of the Victorian Empire); or Richard Hughes *A High Wind in Jamaica* (in which the author simply turns the Victorian view of childhood upside down: the Bas-Thornton children are such fiends that even the pirates who capture them are shocked; but there is still an angel hidden in each.)

It should be noted that Golding's *LoF* is set against the foil of a European atomic war. Unlike Robinson Crusoe who stems from a peaceful world, a stable, optimistic, morally sound British background, firmly rooted in the Christian faith, the children in Golding's book are catapulted onto their island out of a world at war, a world of officers, megaphones, aeroplanes, and flames.
After these introductory considerations the students' attention could be shifted to the more adventurous aspects of an emergency crash landing on an unknown and uninhabited island. Supposing a modern jumbo jet transporting a load of British schoolboys away from danger (cf. "Kinderlandverschickung" in World War II in Nazi Germany, and similarly the evacuation of children from London and from other endangered cities and industrial areas in Great Britain to more rural parts, such as North Wales or the Lake District or even to Australia), got into trouble over some South Sea island and was forced to make a crash landing. The children survive and find themselves in a Robinson Crusoe-like situation. What problems would they be confronted with? In the discussion of this question mention should be made of their need of water, food, shelter, clothes, sanitation. Beyond the satisfaction of these basic needs, however, the boys would have to tackle the organization of their life on the island. The problems to be solved in this context should be listed (water would have to be fetched, collected in vessels, made available; food would have to be provided and prepared; firewood would have to be gathered, fire would have to be lit, main-

tained, looked after; shelters would have to be planned, built, kept up, etc.)
Among the many other possible tasks that might be mentioned could be an exploration of the island and a consideration of rescue measures. Ultimately, a certain order would have to be maintained on the island, possibly a "speaker" to be chosen, (or elected by vote), teams assigned to various jobs and duties. In short: the basics of a miniature democracy would have to be established.
Within this context the students could be asked to describe a typical South Sea island, so that some of the vocabulary needed later on can already be introduced at this early point (e.g.: jungle creepers, undergrowth, trunks, palm trees, coconuts, coral reef, lagoon). The students would then be told that the novel they are to read and discuss in the weeks ahead, W. Golding's *Lord of the Flies,* starts from exactly that type of initial situation: British schoolboys wrecked on a coral island while being evacuated from the European theatre of war.
The reading in class of the opening of the novel is meant to set the key for a good understanding of *Lord of the Flies.* The subsequent discussion of the first passage (Ch. Ia) does not aim at determining an "exposition" in the usual sense of the word. The didactic purpose is just to understand the initial situation the boys find themselves in, to contrast the island setting with the outside world at war, and to give a first characterization of Ralph and the fat boy.

## Plan of the Lesson

*Step 1:*
*Introduction of the topic*

Brief class discussion (island adventure books / Robinson Crusoe / survival on an uninhabited island) leading to an imagined situation (evacuation / plane crash / wrecked on a South Sea Island). Introduction of relevant vocabulary.

*Step 2:*
*The initial situation*

a) After the explanation of some hard words (scar, the Home Counties, casual, crouch) the teacher reads out the opening of the novel (Ch. Ia) trying to bring the situation to life as much as possible.
b) Classroom discussion of the initial situation. A simple board diagram reflects the two worlds mentioned in the text.

*Step 3:*
*Technicalities concerning the reading of the novel and working procedures*

If *LoF* is the first novel for the students to read they will have to be prepared for *extensive reading*. The teacher explains how much reading the students will be expected to do from one course meeting to the next, in what way they should read, and what help they will be given.

The division of the book into four main parts and the subdivision of the 12 chapters into smaller parts should be commented on. To save time the sub-parts of each chapter could be announced by the teacher or listed on a hand-out. The subparts of Chapter I should be dictated to be marked in the book right away. The students will write down a headline, or a brief summary for every part (= standing assignment); this will support their own memory and will eventually give them a comprehensive summary of the whole novel. The passages to be read and prepared intensively will be specially mentioned; guiding questions will accompany the homework accordingly.

The *Vocabulary Annotations* (p. 126–p. 142) are distributed. These include explanations of many terms, colloquialisms, schoolboy slang expressions, and hard words that the students may not know. This will save them a lot of time, and ensure a better understanding of the text; however only the most difficult words and phrases have been explained, so that an occasional reference to an English-English dictionary should be encouraged, too, especially for the passages assigned for close reading.
The students are told how to make their own book-mark with a lines-counter on it to facilitate quotations (cf. p. 12).

*Homework:*
As this is their first contact with the book and the students will have to get used to extensive reading it is advisable not to ask more of them than to read Chapter I at one sitting, the more so as there is rather a lot of unusual vocabulary for them to deal with. They are to write a headline, or a brief summary for each of the eight parts of Chapter I.

## Lesson 2: The Summons of the Conch

### Didactic Considerations

The students have now read the whole of the first chapter of the novel. They can now answer questions within a wider context and yet be made to look at important passages in detail.
It will be interesting to see how the children reveal themselves in their actions. To begin with, Ralph's enchantment with the beauty of his paradisiac surroundings can be contrasted with Piggy's concern and rationale, and later on the arrival of the other children following the summons of the conch encourages us to talk about their various school uniforms and their corresponding colour schemes, the happy mixture of a multitude of colours, so utterly different from the group to arrive next.
The relevance of the finding of the conch and the meaning the shell acquires should be the thematic centre of the lesson. "The Sound of the Shell" provides the title for the opening chapter, which underlines its central importance. The function of the conch should be followed up through the second chapter, as it becomes increasingly clearer.

### Plan of the Lesson

*Step 1:*
*Description of the island and analysis of the initial situation*

After a brief repetition recalling the situation at the beginning of the novel, the description of the setting (beach, platform, pool etc.) might be used for a first brief illustrative sketch. This could be attempted by students on the board, and might be supported by an overhead projector transparency prepared by the teacher.
(Note: This transparency should only show the setting that is known so far. In a second transparency, overlapping the first one, the island geography could be supplemented in the following lesson and,

with a third transparency – placed over the first two – the "map" could be completed later on.)
The students should draw some conclusions with regard to the remote island position, the choice of boys as characters, and the level of meaning suggested by the overall setting.

*Step 2:*
*Characterization of Ralph and Piggy*

The description and characterization of Ralph and the fat boy is carried one step further. Students read p. 10, l. 31 – p. 12, l. 19. Classroom discussion. Board diagram, left hand side. (The right hand side is to be added in the following lesson.)

*Step 3:*
*The conch*

The students discuss the finding of the shell, Piggy's and Ralph's reaction to it, and the meaning it acquires. P. 17, l. 30 – p. 18, l. 22 is read out.

*Step 4:*
*The children obeying the call*

This part (Ch. Id) can be summed up cursorily, with emphasis on the colourful variety of the individual children and their multicoloured apparel. The lesson should be rounded off with a discussion of the implications of this first gathering summoned by the call of the conch: what initiative ought to be taken towards some reasonable organization of the boys' castaway situation?

*Homework:*
The students are asked to prepare Ch. Ie intensively.

## Lesson 3: Steps Towards Democratic Order

### Didactic Considerations

It is important that the first chapter of *LoF* should be well read and understood, as it presents the basis from which the boys attempt their establishment of a democratic system according to the rules they are familiar with.
To begin with the students should comment on Jack's and his choir boys' first appearance, and notice how the consistent imagery of blackness contrasts with the previous arrival of the other children. From the start it is impressed upon the reader that there are two different groups of boys on the island.
Then, attention should be drawn to the importance of the children's assembly, as it is here that the boys take their first steps towards a democratic order; it is essential to note in what manner the first meeting takes place, as there are more assemblies to follow which will be contrasted with the initial one. The boys vote for a chief, but to most of them this is just a game. That the vote also constitutes a struggle for power between Ralph and Jack is obvious from Jack's reactions, and will become clearer before long. What happens after the boys have elected their leader? How do we expect them to organize their life now? What logical sequence of activities would suggest itself? And what do the boys actually do?
If a double period is available, an analysis of the boys' expedition should be included (cf. Step 4, optional).
The expedition (the first of several expeditions in the book) helps to round off the island topography, and shows the boys' continuing enchantment and exhilaration.

At the same time there is an affinity between delirious boyish exuberance and a tendency towards destruction (the rock rolling) that should also be noted.
In a way, the piglet episode epitomises the boys' initial situation on the island. British schoolboys with their civilized upbringing find themselves turned into little Robinson Crusoes, full of adventurous spirit, but innocent, and without the nerve to kill a living animal.
A summing up of Chapter I should show if the students have grasped that in the paradise, the "realized ambition" of the boys' situation, there lurk some shadows, and that there are quite a few ambiguities even in the boys' games. Some critical observations with regard to the children's behaviour, and the discussion of necessary requirements for the development of democratic community life conclude the lesson.
As there is a lot of ground to be covered in this lesson the four parts should be dealt with in great concentration. A double period would allow a more relaxed procedure. All the same, some short illustrative passages should be read out. If time runs short the summing up of the whole chapter could be left to the beginning of the next lesson.

## Plan of the Lesson

*Step 1:*
*Headlines*

As the students have the standing assignment to sum up the parts of a chapter in one or two sentences they should be given the opportunity, either at the beginning of a lesson or in the course of the discussions, to read out their "headlines". These could be written down on the side of the board, or incorporated into the board diagrams.

*Step 2:*
*Description of Jack Merridew and his choir boys*

Students read out p. 20, l. 27 – p. 21, l. 13. The description of Jack and his group is contrasted with the boys around Ralph. When the students characterize Jack, the board diagram from Lesson 2 (written on a transparency) could be displayed again and completed by writing Jack's characteristics next to Ralph's and Piggy's, thus making the contrasting features obvious. Later in the lesson Jack and Ralph could be characterized further by writing down "KNIFE" under Jack's column, and "CONCH" under Ralph's; and also juxtaposing "chief" and "hunter".

*Step 3:*
*Analysis of the boys' election of a chief*

The classroom analysis of the voting procedure and of why Ralph is elected "chief" is supported by references to the text and by having a student read out p. 24, l. 4–14. Jack's reaction must be discussed as it is the key to an understanding of his later behaviour. (The students incorporate their answers to the two homework questions in the discussion.) Before discussing the events after the election, the class is asked to state their ideas as to what the boys ought to do first in their endeavour to establish a working order.

*Step 4: (optional)*
*The "expedition" considered as a sequence of games*

Discussion of the boys' happiness when exploring the island. Students read out a short typical passage (p. 29, l. 1–20).

Analysis of the rock-rolling episode. Quotation of the most important lines (p. 30, l. 12–20). Completion of the map of the island (according to the description on p. 31); either drawn on the board or on a transparency. (Could be supplemented with explanations under the illustration = word field.) Time permitting, the greater part of the piglet episode should be read out by a student (p. 32, l. 32 – p. 34, end) and then be discussed.

*Step 5:*
*Summing up Chapter I*

Looking back over the whole of the first chapter the students sum up the boys' delight at their glamorous new surroundings and the promise of an adventurous playful life, make a short analysis of the games the boys play, and also note some of the ambiguities in the boys' games. Finally, a discussion of indispensable requirements for the development of a democratic community life (in contrast to the boys' actual behaviour) concentrates the students' attention on the essential issue.

*Homework:*
The students are asked to read Chapters II and III, getting them used to an extensive reading of longer parts of a novel. Their special attention is drawn to the development of the second assembly, and particularly to Ralph's handling of the meeting as a chief. The assignment (possibly on a voluntary basis) to draw a "map" of the island topography as known so far should not only be a motivating element, but also prompt the students to read the relevant passages with greater attention, so that later on they will be able to follow the movement of the boys with more familiarity. (To save time in class, they could draw their map on a transparency.)

## Lesson 4: "Democracy" at Work

### Didactic Considerations

While in Chapter I the setting and the overall situation has been established, Chapter II answers the question of how the boys attempt to draw up an autonomous organization of their island existence.
In this lesson the main interest lies in the development of the boys' second assembly, which is a foreshadowing of the course of events on the island later on, especially when seen against the foil of the first assembly. The meeting begins with all the promise of "parliamentary" order, but ends in turmoil. The students should note how Ralph's organized beginning, and the logical sequence of his first statements is continually interrupted and counterfoiled by irrational elements. These come partly from Ralph himself (e.g. when he disregards the more serious thoughts prompted by Piggy and gives in to naive adventure-book emotions) and partly from outside (e.g. from Jack's unrestrained temper which casts a sinister light on most of what he says or does; or from the little boy's fear of a "beastie".)

Thus the analysis of Ch. II a–c should show that the boys' first parliamentary efforts are still very feeble, in spite of the fact that the boys are agreed on their need for hunters, need for rules, and need for a signal fire.

## Plan of the Lesson

*Step 1:*
*The parliamentary platform*

When characterizing the assembly platform, the triangular form of the seating arrangement on the platform should be noted, with the choir boys sitting at Ralph's right, the other larger boys at his left, and the little ones in front. Ralph is sitting with his back to the lagoon. (A more detailed description of the assembly triangle is given later, in Ch. V, p. 84f.) This clearly ordered grouping allows for democratic debates and discussions. – The platform triangle that seems so ideally suited for parliamentary discourse offers an opportunity to illustrate briefly the island topography of which it is a part. Two or three students display their "maps" of the island on transparencies they have prepared at home (or make sketches on the board).
The teacher may decide to have the class list some relevant vocabulary along with the map of the island, as this vocabulary will be used throughout the discussion of the book.
As the first point of Ralph's report refers to the island geography, the link with the analysis of the second meeting is easily established.

*Step 2:*
*Discussion of Ralph's report and his handling of the second meeting*

The students sum up what happens in the three parts of the second assembly; the teacher writes down a few cues. Then Ch. IIa (p. 35 – p. 38, l. 22) should be read out, and analysed intensively.
Ralph's handling of the meeting is worth tracing: Ralph has yet to learn how to be "chief". Quite often the impulses for what Ralph has got to say come from Piggy. Obviously Ralph's qualities of leadership need developing. It would be rewarding to take a close look at Ralph's findings, and Piggy's and Jack's comments, sentence by sentence.

*Step 3:*
*The effect of the "beastie" story on the children*

The little boy's "beastie" story (Ch. IIb) can be discussed quickly; Ralph's desperate attempt to fight the irrational fear that suddenly breaks out in the children should be noted.

*Step 4:*
*The outcome of the second meeting*

This part (Ch. IIc) can also be dealt with quickly; the boys' enthusiasm for a signal fire should be stressed, and finally their light-hearted forgetfulness of the rules.
The mentioning of "the Queen" allows speculations as to the time when the action is supposed to take place: if the "Queen" is Queen Elizabeth II the time could be the near future. (Q.E. II came to the throne in 1952, *LoF* was published in 1954.)
An arrow on the board diagram shows how the organized beginning of the meeting ends in the disorganized breaking up of the assembly.

*Assignments:*
Two assignments could now be given to students: to report on: R. M. Ballantyne's *The Coral Island,* and D. Defoe's *Robinson Crusoe* on the basis of the texts on p. 120ff.
Two students could be asked to do the same assignment each (possibly in pair work); their papers should be completed within two weeks.

## Lesson 5: The Fire

### Didactic Considerations

The main attention in this lesson should be directed towards the fire on the mountain as the symbolic core of this chapter. The students are to realize that the fire the boys intend to light on the mountain top is highly suggestive of the light of human reason and is thus a symbol of hope and survival. However, to Ralph, Jack and almost all the other boys, their life on the island, their "rules" and projects, are still primarily a sequence of games to be enthusiastically – and unthinkingly – enjoyed. Everything is done on the spur of the moment, in childish exuberance and ignorance, without consideration of possible consequences. The outcome of their actions invariably takes them by surprise. The fire they eventually light is endowed with a sinister ambiguity when it gets out of control and instead of being a torch of hope reaching out for rescue, turns into a token of destruction. Thus the boys' youthful irresponsibility repeatedly results in a movement from order to near-chaos.
The students should realize the implications of Ralph's expressing the need for more rules, supported by Jack's "We've got to have rules and obey them." Both Ralph and Jack are aware of the fact that they have got to "do the right things". But will they? How convincing is Jack's naive confidence in the English being "best at everything"?
The only one to display some rationale and forethought is Piggy, the boy the others laugh at and tease most of the time. Piggy's tirade and the implications of what he says (a warning as well as a premonition) should be a point of special interest.

### Plan of the Lesson

*Step 1:*
*The game of preparing the fire*

Students read out p. 43, l. 12–29 and comment on the delirious and unthinking way the boys go about collecting wood for the signal fire. Also of great significance is the sense of "togetherness" the boys display when all of them share the same burden, as the glamour of these communal efforts strongly contrasts with later events.

*Step 2:*
*First failures*

Without much loss of time the analysis of this passage should concentrate on the connection between the boys' exuberant excitement and their lack of forethought and consideration, and on the fact that they do not consider the fire to be a vital means of rescue and a symbol of their desire for survival, but rather sèe it as just another thrilling game to be enjoyed.
The boys' innocent joyful dancing when the fire has been lit should be mentioned, as it will soon change dramatically with the intrusion of ritual elements.

*Step 3:*
*Fire out of control*

Detailed discussion of Piggy's indignant "tirade" and its implications. Students read p. 49, l. 1 – p. 51, end.

*Step 4:*
*Tracing main developments in Chapter II*

The students sum up in a few words the main results found in the last two lessons.

*Homework:*
The class is divided into two groups, both of which are to re-read Chapter III, but with their attention directed towards different character analyses. Group 1 is to study Jack in IIIa, and compare and contrast Jack with Ralph in IIIb; Group 2 is to study Simon in IIIb, and compare and contrast Simon with Jack in IIIa. The students are to make notes of their observations and will be asked to report their findings in the next lesson.

## Lesson 6: Three Boys and Their Ways

### Didactic Considerations

In Chapter III Golding develops the characteristics of Jack, Ralph, and Simon in three clearly distinguishable passages, relating to three typical situations. The significant differences between these three boys should be analysed; the findings from this chapter will be necessary for an understanding of later developments. Emphasis should be laid on the last passage (IIIc), as Simon is so clearly contrasted with the other boys, especially with Jack. As IIIa and IIIc are entirely descriptive and deliberately ornate, they are not easy to read, and it may be necessary for the teacher to refer the students to revealing phrases or sentences. To facilitate the proceedings, students from the two groups designated for the homework should report their findings and thus divide the lesson into three parts. Attention should be drawn to the point of view from which the three passages are narrated: Jack and Ralph (in IIIa and b) are seen mainly from outside, from the third person narrator's point of view. In the course of IIIc the point of view is changing, when Simon creeps into his jungle cabin, and the reader experiences his surroundings through Simon's senses, as it were.

### Plan of the Lesson

According to their assignments two of the students from each group report on their findings regarding the characterization of the three boys and their ways in Chapter III, possibly incorporating observations on the boys' development from the beginning up to this point.

*Step 1:*
*Jack – the hunter*

Although not easy to read for students, at least part of the description of Jack going after pigs in fanatic absorption should be read out, possibly by the teacher himself (p. 52 to p. 53, l. 2); then two students characterize Jack in his dedication and compulsion to hunt and kill.

*Step 2:*
*The hunter and the home-builders*

The two students go on to report their findings concerning the contrast between Jack and Ralph, before the rest of the group contribute further observations. Then p. 56 – p. 57, l. 5 is read out by a student. This is followed up by some further corroborating questions from the teacher.

*Step 3:*
*Simon – the mystic*

Two students from Group 2 characterize Simon, under special consideration of the surroundings in which Simon is described.

Then Simon is compared and contrasted with Jack, which should reveal the most extreme contrast of personality and character represented by these two boys.

*Step 4: (optional)*
*Structure and point of view in Chapter III*

The clear structure of Chapter III lends itself to a brief analysis and so does Golding's handling of the point of view, i.e. the outlook that the author assumes in narrating his story. The students should be made to notice how time and again (especially in IIIa and IIIc) the narrator who sees and records events from outside, from a neutral distance, becomes the "omniscient author" who slips into the mind of his characters and experiences their surroundings through their senses.

*Homework:*
Extensive reading of Chapters IV, V and VI.
Intensive preparation of IVb.
The topics of Student Papers Nos. 3, 4, 5 and 6, (cf. p. 111) are announced and assigned (to two students each).

## Chapters IV to VI: "Things are breaking up."

The students have read Chapters IV, V and VI as one sequence and are aware of the decline of the children's organized society, and of their growing fear of a "beast". It will therefore be possible from now on to put some of the episodes into a wider perspective by tracing the development of themes, motifs, or symbolism over several chapters, although it will remain indispensable to concentrate on selected passages, or "scenes", to accentuate the steps in the development. The three chapters will be discussed in four sessions under the general aspect (to be determined by the students) "Things are Breaking up", concentrating in Lesson 7 on the revealing display of natural childish aggressiveness and its meaning in view of social conditioning; in Lesson 8 on the regressive tendencies to be observed in Jack and his hunters, and on the symbolism of Jack's knife as contrasted with Piggy's glasses; in Lesson 9 on the development of the meetings; and in Lesson 10 on a comparison of the two excursions.

## Lesson 7: Natural Belligerence Versus Social Conditioning

### Didactic Considerations

Just as the first three chapters of *LoF* form a coherent unit, Chapter IV introduces another unit of three chapters in which the birth of evil is shown when irresponsibility becomes viciousness, and violence is inflicted on a fellow human being. A generalizing description of the pattern of the boys' daily island existence provides the connecting link, and at the same time creates a sense of time passing. It should be spoken about briefly. The classroom discussion in this lesson should however concentrate on Chapter IVb, which is one of the most revealing passages of the whole book.
The students should consider the way in which the "natural belligerence" of tiny "innocent" tots is triggered off by the inexplicably aggressive behaviour of only slightly bigger children; how even the

peaceful absorption of the smallest boys in their games contains an irrational element when they enjoy the exercise of control over living things; and how easily "teasing" (Roger's stone throwing) might become torture.
As on the other hand the older boys are checked in their behaviour by the "taboo of the old life", the question that results concerns the relevance of social conditioning as opposed to innate natural drives. How thick is the veneer of civilization? What is the basis that civilization is founded on? How much sense does it make to rely on this basis if Western civilization has so often proved frail and now, too, lies in "ruins"? The students could be made to realize that in IVc an answer is given to these questions when in imitation of war techniques ("dazzle paint") Jack hides his face behind a mask and thus releases himself from shame and self-consciousness. It is Jack's adoption of modern warfare camouflage that starts him off on his reversion to savagery.

## Plan of the Lesson

*Step 1:*
*"Things are breaking up."*

A brief 'brainstorming' is undertaken to establish the general tendency of the sequence of the three chapters to be analysed.

*Step 2:*
*Sand and stone throwing: The development of inexplicable violence*

The class is given a few minutes to look at p. 65, l. 7 – p. 68, l. 4 again, as this is one of the crucial passages of the book. (Alternative: IVb is read out by a student.) It is in this sequence of scenes that the ambivalence of the children's games as observed so far comes notably to the fore, i.e. their inherent aggression as well as a restraining force that – as yet – conditions them. The students can look backward and forward in the chapters of *LoF* that they have read so far and comment on the influence of societal factors ("civilization") on the boys' behaviour.

*Step 3:*
*Liberation through camouflage: Jack's mask*

In direct connection with the question of social conditioning countered by acts of inexplicable violence, the students are asked to comment on the special significance of Jack's mask and the immediate (taboo-breaking) effect it has.

*Homework:*
Increasingly, the students should be made to consider *LoF* in terms of correspondences and developments. Therefore their assignment to trace the changes in Jack and his choirboys is meant to open their eyes to the gradual deterioration of the civilized element on the island.

# Lesson 8: The Knife and the Glasses

## Didactic Considerations

In Lessons 8 to 10 the students will realize the distance we have covered from the beginning of the book; especially in this lesson when considering the change Jack and his demure choir boys have undergone, but also in the next when the development of the three assemblies will be recapitulated, and in the following lesson, when the two expeditions are compared.

After a brief discussion of the irony of the fact that the ship (promising rescue) slowly passes by on the horizon as Jack's hunters have abandoned their responsibilities and let the signal fire go out while killing their first pig, the students' attention is focused on the development of Jack Merridew from his first appearance to this moment, and on the weapons that characteristically have accompanied him from the start (knife and stick). The students comment on the change in Jack's choir boys and on the implications Jack's blood-smeared hands and the repeated mention of blood evoke.

Jack's development is contrasted with the position Ralph finds himself in now. The threat to an orderly organization of the boys' civilization on the island through a loss of self-control as can be observed from the start should be stressed in an analysis of Chapter IVe where the growing antagonism between Jack and Ralph comes to a point where Jack vents his aggressions by lashing out at Piggy (who has been siding with Ralph all along) and breaking Piggy's glasses. The symbolic significance of the glasses in contrast to the knife should be recognized.

The final part of the chapter with the boys' regression to the ritual game of an imitation pig hunt should be included in the discussion, as it contains further hints at a development in a direction detrimental to civilized order and disciplined behaviour.

## Plan of the Lesson

*Step 1:*
*Jack Merridew: From choir boy prefect to bloodthirsty hunter*

The appearance of Jack and his group of hunters from the "unfriendly side", in procession, stimulates a comparison with the first arrival of the choir boys. Incorporating their homework findings, the students trace revealing elements in Jack's development, such as his emphatic knife stabbing p. 26, 2; 33,3; 33,16; 34,1; 77,21; 80,7; his delirious rock rolling; his breaking up of assemblies, thus disobeying the rules; his compulsive hunting (considering barbs on spears for more effective slaughter (p. 56), thinking of the pigs' most likely resting places (p. 58), having the idea of "dazzle paint" to "creep up and stab" (p. 69), of using sticks as spears and stakes, etc.) Jack's first kill and the implications of the blood on his hands (and his reaction to it) will have to be carefully analysed. (The main steps in Jack Merridew's development from chapter chorister to bloodthirsty hunter could be traced in a transparency prepared for this lesson; only the column on the right-hand side would have to be filled in in class.)

*Step 2:*
*Growing antagonism between Jack and Ralph*

Jack's ecstatic behaviour in IVe must be linked with Ralph's discovery of the dead signal fire in IVd and his despair at Jack's neglect of his communal obligations. From the start Jack is contrasted with Ralph but also with Piggy (cf. Piggy's suggestion to use a stick as a sundial to Jack's use of a stick as a "spear" and a "stake"), whose glasses are just as important and suggestive as Jack's knife.

P. 76, l. 22 to p. 78, l. 9 should be read out, preceding a close text analysis of IVe.

*Steps 3 and 4:*
*The knife and the glasses / The circles*

Whereas the symbolic significance of the conch has already been analysed sufficiently, the connotations evoked by Jack's knife and Piggy's glasses should now be defined by students from the group assigned this question.
Likewise, if more briefly, the meaning of the circles mentioned in IVf should be analysed by the students assigned this question.

*Homework:*
Attention is drawn to the boys' clearest political instrument, their assemblies, and the general tendency that becomes apparent in them, as this will be the central topic of the next lesson.

## Lesson 9: Rational Action Versus Irrational Action: The Third Assembly

### Didactic Considerations

As Golding develops his story he employs a technique of repetition and contrast, the later chapters of the novel repeating the structure of the first. Comparing the meetings, the students should notice that the third assembly, which takes up the whole of Chapter V, repeats the pattern of the second assembly in Chapter II, if under different conditions. ("This meeting must be business, not fun.") The third assembly is of special significance as in its course the boy's precarious situation between order (daylight sanity) and succumbing to dark emotions is convincingly established. The movement from order to chaos, so generally apparent now in almost everything the boys undertake, can be traced again. Once more Ralph's attempt to restore order and reorganize the boys finally fails and his faith in democracy dwindles, as once more the assembly is broken up by Jack.
The students should be allowed time in class to go through Chapter V again and note down the various stages and speakers of the meeting, and to recognize the common denominator that constantly disturbs a sane conduct of the proceedings: irrational fear. (They should also pay attention to the effect that darkness and nightfall have on the meeting.) Finally, a recapitulation of the development of the first three assemblies could shed a light on the general course the island boat is steering. The shouts of enthusiasm and excitement of the first island days have changed to the wail of nightmares and the incantation of savage ritual.
A student paper (No. 3: Rational Action versus Irrational Action in Chapters I to VI) could be incorporated when discussing the intrusion of irrational elements in the assemblies; it would sum up the instability of the situation the children find themselves in, and would show how the boys constantly counteract their own original intentions.

*Optional:*

An analysis of how the boys are gradually taken over and dominated by irrational fear might be added at this point. This development could be traced in Chapters I to V, from the first mention of a "snake-thing" (p. 39) that chills the boys, makes them "restless" and produces "grave nodding", to the end of Ch. V where there is fear everywhere: Piggy is in a state of fear, as he is scared of Jack; there are screams of "real terror" from the boys' "game"/ritual on the beach; the littluns are afraid of the dark and have nightmares; Ralph and Piggy are depressed by their realization that "things are drifting" and "rotten".

*Alternative:*

Especially if a double period is available: Student Papers No 1 and/or No 2 could be read out; familiarity with the plot of Defoe's *Robinson Crusoe* and Ballantyne's *The Coral Island* would enable the students to follow the development of the action in *LoF* with greater awareness of the inherent differences from the two well-known island adventure books.

## Plan of the Lesson

*Step 1:*
*Analysis of the third meeting*

The students are given five minutes to go through Chapter V again and note the various stages, and speakers, of the third meeting (pair work). The results are then formulated and discussed. A few short passages should be quoted, such as Piggy's rational arguing (p. 91, l. 12–24) and his bombastic statement "Life is scientific", or Simon's effort to express himself (p. 97, l. 6–34). (The left-hand side of the board diagram could be prepared on a transparency, to save time, so that only the notes on the right-hand side would have to be filled in in class.)

*Step 2:*
*The development of the first three assemblies: rational versus irrational action*

Drawing on their homework notes the students briefly trace significant elements noticeable in the meetings from the start, but more clearly revealed now. They should consider the original intention of all three meetings, and realize the factors that counteract these intentions. In this context Student Paper No. 3, tracing the development of rational action versus irrational action in Chapters I to VI, is read out, discussed and supplemented by the group. The student who reads his paper out should list his points in two columns on a transparency, which he himself could add to if the class has further contributions.
*Homework:*
Chapter VI should be reread, and VIc prepared intensively. The two guiding questions are assigned as oral homework to two groups – each specializing on one.

# Lesson 10: The "Beast" – Product of Human Imagination

## Didactic Considerations

It is important for the students to understand the ironical message of the "sign from the world of grown-ups", and its connection with the boys' fear of a "beast". They must realize how and why the belief in a beast comes into existence. They should recognize that the twins' "dreadful news" stems from their own frightened imagination (later on to be contrasted with Simon's fearless "good news"); and that the other boys accept

Samneric's story of the presence of a beast because they are themselves in a state of fear.
Another objective of this lesson is for the class to become aware of the pattern of parallelism and contrast employed by the author. The second expedition evokes memories of the first exploration of the island, but this time the boys are not filled with the enthusiasm of that first glamorous day. They are now exploring "the other side" of the island, and the students should become aware of the symbolism of the two sides of the island, the protected "good" side with the lagoon, and the unprotected, dangerously wild side, the latter underscored by the comparison with the sleeping "leviathan", the evil Biblical monster. (Student Paper No. 4 should be incorporated.) It is at the end of the chapter, i.e. at the end of the first half of the book, that the boys cross this border line. The students should comment on the boys' half-delirious rock rolling and compare it to their first games at the beginning, to reveal the sinister undertones that have crept in.
Rounding off the first half of the book, a student paper (No. 5) could now be read out and discussed examining the symbolism of the island geography.

## Plan of the Lesson

*Step 1:*
*The "sign" from the world of grown-ups*

Brief classroom analysis of the significance of the dead parachutist falling onto the mountain top. Quotation of p. 104, l. 24 to p. 105, l. 9.

*Step 2:*
*The "beast"*

Discussing the important question of the origin of "beast" and fear, the students are asked to put themselves into the boys' situation and to consider how they would have reacted in their place. They should realize that the boys' fear is rooted entirely in their own imagination, and not in anything outside them.

*Step 3:*
*Hunting the beast*

Analysis of the second expedition in comparison with the first. The students read out their homework, or make their contributions based on the homework questions, pointing out both parallels and contrasts between the two expeditions. When the passage describing the "sleeping leviathan" is discussed (it should be read by a student) this offers an opportunity for Student Report No. 4 to be included (Summary information on Th. Hobbes' philosophical treatise *The Leviathan;* p. 125.) As Hobbes will be referred to again in the final discussion, this report should be very concise and merely informative.
The comparison between the two expeditions is then continued with an analysis of the different sides of the island explored, and with a closer look at the "games" played on both occasions. It should become clear that at the end of Chapter VI Ralph can only just maintain order and assert his leadership, and that there is a precarious balance at the end of the first half of *LoF.*

*Step 4:*
*The symbolism of the island geography*

As the comparison of the two sides of the island has already touched on some points of symbolic significance, the lesson could be rounded off with Student Paper No. 5 interpreting possible levels of meaning of the island geography. (Transparency)

*Homework:*
Extensive reading of Chapters VII-IX. Student Papers Nos. 7, 8, 9 and 10 are assigned (to two students each). (Cf. p. 111f.)

## Chapters VII to IX: "We are going to have fun on this island!"

In Chapters VII to IX Golding demonstrates how the nature of the boys accounts for the nature and the growth of the evil that takes over in all of them, except Simon. The action of these three chapters converges in the first dreadful climax when the power of darkness manifests itself in the killing of Simon.
The analysis of Chapters VII to IX had best take place in two phases (if possible: two double periods); the first dealing with Ch. VII and the first part of Ch. VIII, the second with the rest of Ch. VIII and Ch. IX. In Ch. VII and VIIIa–c the main interest lies on Ralph and Jack, whose characteristics are developed further in a highly significant way. Ch. VIIId–f and Ch. IX focus on Simon and the Lord of the Flies.

## Lessons 11/12: "Daylight Sanity" and Anarchic Impulses

### Didactic Considerations

These two periods (ideally a double period) concentrate on the various aspects of the boys' conflict between adhering to civilized behaviour and yielding to primitive instincts. The two focal points are on Ralph and on Jack respectively, as their characteristics are developed further in some telling situations. For the first time Ralph is carried away by a sudden anarchic impulse himself. The only one to be disgustedly aware of the boys' growing lack of concern about filth, who nostalgically daydreams of the Paradise Lost of his earlier childhood back home, he is suddenly caught by a "thick excitement" in the pig hunt and also in the savage dance afterwards! What does this reveal about Ralph's nature? The students should realize how little it takes to liberate the destructive instincts that apparently lie only skin-deep even in "responsible" human beings.
Important though this observation is, it should be discussed in direct connection with Ralph's bad conscience as displayed after the "game", which indicates that his set of values is still intact, whereas Jack's response reveals a frightening loss of conscience.
Clearly, though, Ralph too shows flaws in this chapter, and these should be analysed. His being "less skilful" than before on their way up to the mountain top (VII d) is meaningful. He allows Jack to provoke him into unreasonable action, and in almost complete physical and spiritual darkness eventually succumbs to his own fearful imagination and (like the twins) believes he sees the "beast" on the moun-

tain top when, in actual fact, he is only confronted with the sight of the dead parachutist. Once again the students should realize that the boys create their own monsters (ape-like creature!), and thus instead of steering a course of rationalism, order and enlightenment, move backwards to superstition and inchoate fears.

When we turn our attention from Ralph to Jack to observe Jack's development from hunter to tribal "chief", the conflict between rational and irrational action is stressed further.

The students should reflect on the immediate effect of Jack's cutting himself off from "Ralph's lot", as more and more boys desert Ralph to join Jack. The initial grouping of the first chapters is thus significantly carried one step further. There are going to be two groups on the island from now on: the 'hut-builders and home-seekers' near the platform by the lagoon, and the tribe of the hunters near the rocky end of the island. A precarious unity has now been split into two fundamentally different camps. The question to be considered is for what reason Ralph is deserted by so many boys, and why they did not openly dare to side with Jack when he asked them to.

The last part of Chapter VIII, the killing of the sow, should be analysed intensively, as it contains the answer to some of the questions raised, revealing that the option which Jack offers, and which appeals to the deserters, is anarchic freedom, the opposite of democratic, responsible, reasonable behaviour.

## Plan of the Lesson

*Step 1:*
*Civilized standards and instinctive action*

In a brief opening discussion Ralph's behaviour in Chapters VII and VIII is analysed as oscillating between sane, civilized action and surrender to instinctive impulses. These two sides of Ralph's nature are followed up in some revealing scenes. The key passage of Ralph's participation in the mock hunt, p. 126, l. 14–34, is read out by a student. The fact that under the given circumstances Ralph, too, succumbs to dark aggressive instincts is discussed.

*Step 2:*
*Ralph's loss of "skill"*

The students find further instances of Ralph's decreasing skill with regard to his physical and moral qualities, which implies his leadership qualities as well. The "black curtain" that frequently blots his mind out changes into physical and spiritual blindness when (at the end of Ch. VII) Ralph, too, believes in "seeing" the beast.

*Step 3:*
*Compulsion and conscience*

As in Step 1, the students are asked first of all to give a brief account of the "scenes" in which Jack is characterized further. Then, relatively quickly, after a quiet reading of p. 126, l. 27 – p. 127, l. 13, Jack's behaviour in the imitation pig hunt is compared and contrasted to Ralph's, and his ecstasy discussed as foreshadowing later events when Jack will find the fulfilment of his anarchic impulses in the "real" hunt. The students must realize, however, that Jack cannot completely surrender to his instincts as long as he is bound by the rules of Ralph's democratic island organization.

*Step 4:*
*Jack's desertion*

The class is asked to re-read p. 138, 20 – p. 141, 13 and to consider three questions (cf. Stundenblatt), the answers to which are briefly discussed. Then the immediate consequences of Jack's desertion as well as the "political" implications are analysed, possibly with speculations as to the direction in which the boys' island boat will be steering from now on.

*Step 5:*
*The release of primitive instincts*

As the scene of the sow killing represents the first culmination of a development from "daylight sanity" to total surrender to anarchic impulses, it should be read out (p. 147, 27 – p. 149, 28) and looked at closely.
Jack, Roger and the "tribe" can now let "game" become reality. Unlike the occasion of the mock pig hunt (p. 126) they can now stab at, hurt and torment a "real" pig. We record the momentary victory of savage instincts and thus the defeat of sane and civilized action in Jack's tribe.

*Homework:*
Intensive preparation of Chapter VIIIf, IXa and p. 167 – p. 169,10.

## Lessons 13/14: Simon and the "Lord of the Flies"

### Didactic Considerations

The description of Simon's encounter with the Lord of the Flies is one of the most significant parts of Golding's novel as it contains a comment on the power of darkness that gradually takes over. It is the two scenes of Simon's confrontation with the Lord of the Flies that have given the book its title, which underlines their importance. The students should realize the symbolic significance of the "pig's head on a stick" which becomes the "Lord of the Flies", and they should discuss the nature of evil it stands for, the reason why things are "no go" on the island as elsewhere in the world.
Chapter IX must be considered in close connection with the second part of Chapter VIII. It presents a first dreadful climax with the death of Simon who is mistaken for the "beast" and brutally done to death, ironically just at the moment when he is about to bring the boys the "good news" that the "beast" is in fact harmless. The only one to see the reason why things are "no go" on the island, and to grasp the nature of the boys' inner darkness becomes the victim of the mob's fearful violent ecstasy. It is the dire clash of what is described in Chapter IXa with the occurrence in Chapter IXc that should become clear in the discussion.
Simon's death should be interpreted as the climax of anarchic violence. It is the end in a long chain of menacing events, each containing the germ of the next. What begins with Ralph's playfully machine-gunning Piggy in Chapter I is continued in the boys' rock rolling, in Jack's actual killing of a pig, then of a

sow, and his invention of the chant and dance, then in Jack's viciously hitting Piggy. The next step is their "pretending" to beat the boy who acts the part of the pig; mock hunting soon has the sound of "real terror" to it when the excitement of inflicting pain gets out of hand. Simon's killing means that a last barrier has been pulled down; it is the turning point from the dominance of democratic principles to the dominance of anarchy on the island. The students should recognize without difficulty the religious (Christian) implications of Simon's death, and of his disappearance at the end of Chapter IX, which is symbolically steeped in a mysterious light and adds a universal perspective.

## Plan of the Lesson

*Step 1:*
*Simon*

Starting with homework question 1, the situation in the clearing after the killing and paunching of the sow is clarified, especially with regard to the fact that Simon has been watching the whole scene from his cabin. The students recall briefly what it is that has set Simon apart from the other boys in the novel so far, before Simon's confrontation with the pig's head is analysed.

*Step 2:*
*Simon's encounter with the Lord of the Flies*

Simon's confrontation with the LoF is a scene of great importance. It is mystic to a high degree and yet at the same time realistic as well, which makes it difficult to approach. Whereas Golding interrupts the scene with a contrasting episode (Jack's raid of Ralph's fire), it is methodically feasible to consider and discuss the two parts in class as the one coherent unit it actually is.

A generalizing answer to homework question 2, pointing to the two levels of interpretation (realistic and symbolic) should set the framework for the subsequent discussion. The students read quietly through p. 151, 24 to p. 152, 26 again, and then talk about the pig's head's "speaking" to Simon. It is important to note how from now on the flies (displacing the butterflies) become a current symbol of instinctive living which links them (realistically and symbolically) with the pig's head that is now called the LoF.

The term "LoF" should be explained by a student (assignment); its relevance to the book as a whole (importance of the title!) need not be discussed yet at this point. Simon's overcoming the temptation to look away, his clearsighted recognition of the nature of the "beast", and the LoF's most significant sentences in VIIIf are discussed and noted down on the board.

*Optional:*
As a summary of the results of the discussion the text on p. 93 could be handed out, read quietly, and commented on.

*Step 3:*
*Simon's recognition of truth*

The questions listed in the "Stundenblatt" to analyse Simon's ascent of the mountain and recognition of the whole truth, can be dealt with in pairs to provide further methodical variation in a basically discussion-oriented period.

*Steps 4 and 5:*
*The power of darkness / Simon's death*

After a characterization of the situation on the beach before the storm, the stu-

dents read out the crucial passage p. 167 – p. 168, 29 which should then be discussed very intensively.
The ecstatic dance must be recognized as a protective ritual to ward off the boys' fears, and their regression to barbarism as a channelling of their fears on to a scapegoat (= the "beast"). It is deeply ironical that in their blind obsession they kill Simon, as their victim is the one who could have become their saviour.

The climax reached with Simon's death at the end of Chapter IX offers an opportunity to trace briefly the steps that have led up to this point in the novel. Before the last three chapters of *LoF* are read, the students can make their own assumptions as to the further development of the boys' island existence.

**The Encounter between Simon and the Lord of the Flies**

The episode is a symbolic representation of the conflict between the highest and lowest impulses in man. The Lord of the Flies is explaining that there is no sense in trying to hunt and kill the beast. "You knew, didn't you? I'm part of you? Close, close, close! I'm the reason why it's no go? Why things are what they are?" The Lord of the Flies answers the question of why the civilisation of the boys is a failure. The destructive element is in the boys themselves – in each boy.
Is the speech of the Lord of the Flies actually of diabolical origin, or is it a figment of Simon's imagination? It could be either. Simon is prone to fits and possesses an active imagination. At the same time, the Lord of the Flies utters truths that are beyond the knowledge of a mere boy in explaining why things are "no go" on the island. In deliberately leaving indefinite the question of the origin of the Lord of the Flies, Golding seems to be saying that it does not matter what name you give to evil, call it devil, sin, neurosis, hate, violence, brutality; the important fact is that evil exists inside man and is a necessary part of the human condition. The symbolic encounter between Simon and the Lord of the Flies represents the conflict between good and evil as it occurs in every man. And just as Simon and the Lord of the Flies represent universal tendencies, so each of the other characters stands for a single quality – cruelty, destructiveness, creativity, or intellect – which exists to a greater or lesser degree in every man. Analyze any individual and you find in him Ralph's tendency to adventure and to common sense, Piggy's intellectualism, Simon's religious and poetic feelings, Roger's willingness to torture, Jack's appetite for destruction, Samneric's desire to please other people. How these different elements are oriented in the individual decides his moral outlook. But they are all present as impulses in the human personality. Thus, at the same time that *Lord of the Flies* is a novel exploring the disintegration of a society, it is also a study of the identity of man.

From: *F. Jackson,* William Golding, Lord of the Flies, Coles Notes, Toronto 1970, p. 26f.

*Step 6:*
*Simon's disappearance*

Depending on how much time is left, this step can be shortened, although the description of Simon's dead body is extremely suggestive of Christian elements, a fact that could be drawn on to underline the terminology we used before (cf. prophet, saviour).

*Homework:*
The students are asked to read the last part of the novel, Chapters X to XII. For the next period they are expected to be familiar with Chapter X, which the homework question refers to. The question as to how Ralph and Piggy, and Jack and his hunters respectively, react to the killing of Simon, and the assignment to underline the relevant sentences, is meant to save time in the first step of Lesson 15.

## Chapters X to XII: "Never mind what's sense. That's gone."

The last three chapters of the novel could be analysed in two major parts: Chapters X and XI being dominated by the symbols of the conch and the glasses, and culminating in the destruction of the conch and Piggy's death; and Chapter XII demonstrating the complete release of monstrous savagery, and being permeated by the cynical grin of the victorious Lord of the Flies.
First (in Lessons 15 and 16) the students should follow up the symbol of the glasses on the one hand (and the corresponding theme of vision and blindness so often touched upon in the book) and that of the conch on the other. The two symbols are brought together in the person of Piggy who is described as continually cleaning his specs to see more clearly, and who keeps caring for and respecting the conch as the most valuable item on the island. The class will recognize a profound logic in the fact that Piggy's death and the shattering of the conch coincide.
Then (in Lessons 17 and 18) the students trace the events after Piggy's death, analysing Ralph's tragic isolation, considering the meaning of the Lord of the Flies' indestructible grin, and discussing the consequences of Jack's heedless exploitation of irresponsible authority. They follow the ever-increasing savagery of the man-hunt up to the ultimate climax when Ralph is down on his knees expecting the fatal stab. Finally, the class should realize the implications of the unexpected "gimmick" ending as the grinning officer who seems to bring rescue represents only an extension of the evil apparent among the boys on the island.

## Lesson 15: Vision and Blindness

### Didactic Considerations

This lesson deals with various aspects of clearsightedness and blindness, in a physical as well as a figurative sense.
In the first of the three parts of Chapter X, Ralph is the one to clearsightedly face reality, i.e. the murder of Simon, whilst Piggy refuses to accept the fact, defending himself on the grounds of his impaired vision. Sam and Eric, too, do not admit their involvement, although their shame tells on them.
In the second part the fact that the savages flinch away from their individual

memories shows a similar reaction to Piggy's and the twins'. It should be noted, however, how cleverly Jack manages to cloud the boys' vision by turning Simon into a scapegoat, convincing them that killing Simon was the only thing to do, as "the beast disguised itself" and came in his shape.

The theft of Piggy's glasses in the final part of the chapter epitomizes the contrast between, on the one hand: vision, clear-sightedness, ingenuity, fire, warmth, rescue, sanity, and on the other hand: blindness, darkness, fear, nightmares, blind fury, violence.

The students should analyse these different aspects of vision and blindness, and compare and contrast the boys' varying reactions to the first murder on the island. The clear grouping of the boys into two opposing camps invites an analysis of their respective organizations and the political implications.

*Optional:*
The point now reached in the development of the island community lends itself to a review of the various stages in Ralph's leadership; and a consideration of Jack's expedition to steal Piggy's glasses, which parallels the boys' former expeditions, could be used to demonstrate their continuous regression. (Student Paper No. 6)

## Plan of the Lesson

*Step 1:*
*The morning after the feast*

Seeing and looking away (i. e. facing reality and flinching away from it) are forms of "vision" and "blindness"; it is significant that only Ralph accepts his share of guilt frankly, whereas the others, including Piggy (!) display guilty consciences but without admitting their involvement.

*Step 2:*
*The theft of Piggy's glasses*

The students read quietly through p. 183, 28 to p. 184, 33 and the end of the chapter, p. 186, 7–14, again. They will notice the parallels with the frenzied nightly attack on Simon, and should list some of the verbs that reveal the savagery of the fight in the dark. They should realize that Ralph has hit foe and friend alike, e. g. Eric, (cf. p. 184, 25 and p. 185, 21–31) and so has Eric (cf. p. 184, 28 and p. 185, 25). They consider the fact that Jack has no interest whatsoever in the conch any longer, but ruthlessly steals Piggy's glasses to complete his absolute power.

*Step 3:*
*The organization of the two groups*

Jack's total disregard of the immediate consequences of his stealing Piggy's specs, his lack of sympathy with Piggy's blindness, is in itself a telling comment on Jack's Machiavellian leadership attitude. The end that justifies the means for him is his own independence and absolute control. Jack's system is autocratic, dictatorial, tyrannic, totalitarian. The means he uses, accordingly, are those known from such political systems: pressure, strict control, ritualized behaviour, projection and establishment of an enemy image ("the others", the "beast in disguise") [cf. "the Reds" p. 179, 14, who seem to be the enemy in the adult war] – This is to be contrasted with (what is left of) Ralph's democratic system. The board diagram reflects the two "political" groupings on the island.

*Step 4: (optional)*
*Retrospection: the development of Ralph's leadership*

In connection with the analysis of the two "political" systems now established on the island, the distance we have travelled from the beginning could be measured by tracing the various stages in the development of Ralph's leadership (and possibly the gradual parallel usurpation of power by Jack).
The class is divided into two groups, and allowed to deal with the questions in pair work. This should not take up much time, although it means thumbing through the pages again, and jotting down notes. – The questions on the Stundenblatt could be supplemented with questions such as: – Who, in your opinion, is responsible for this development? – How does Jack's development parallel and contrast with Ralph's?

*Step 5: (optional)*
*The four expeditions on the island*

Student Paper No. 6 could be read out in this context, as the development of the boys' "expeditions" reflects the same tendency as observed in the general development of the island community. The student who reads his paper out should have prepared a transparency (cf. p. 114f.).

Steps 4 and 5 could be included if a double period is available; otherwise they might be considered as a possible additional lesson.

## Lesson 16: The Possibilities of Irresponsible Authority

### Didactic Considerations

It is in Chapter XI that the destruction of the ideals of a democratic society is finally and devastatingly presented. The students must realize that the last straw of hope, Piggy's moral imperative ("... you got to!"), has no validity in the face of irresponsible, tyrannical power, and that therefore Ralph's appeal, too, with his pathetic reference to British sportsmanship ("you aren't playing the game") appears almost ludicrous in view of the savages' painted anonymity and their utter disregard of civilized values.
And yet it should also become clear that Piggy's association with the conch, which he so cherishes and carries "against all odds", and his fervent belief in "What's right is right", puts him on a par with Simon. Piggy's final great moment when he says what he has got to say, culminating with "Which is better – to have rules and agree, or to hunt and kill?", trying to convey to the painted savages the essential message of civilization (and summarizing the conflicts in the book) makes him appear almost as much of a seer (blind though he is) as Simon was.
The class should recognize the meaning that lies in the simultaneous destruction of both Piggy and the conch; the shattering of the conch underlining the collapse of democratic order once represented by the shell, and Piggy's broken head indicating the destruction of his brains and intelligence. Just as Simon's death marked the obliteration of imagination and humane vision, Piggy's death marks the end of intellect and reason on the island.

*Optional:*
The end of the chapter, which deals with the ultimate effects of irresponsible authority, draws attention to Roger, the boy who in "delirious abandonment" levers the rock that kills Piggy, and is now described as one "wielding a nameless authority". This offers an opportunity to trace one example of a boy's development from his first appearance to the final stages of the book (Student Paper No. 8: Roger, cf. p. 115).

## Plan of the Lesson

*Step 1:*
*"What's right is right."*

After a brief characterization of the situation Ralph, Piggy and Samneric now find themselves in, all of them "blinded" in one way or the other, attention is focused on what could be called Piggy's moral imperative, his pitiful attempt to rely on "the rules of the games" the boys once learned. The students read out p. 189, 18–33.

*Step 2:*
*"You aren't playing the game."*

The students analyse the contrast between Piggy's illusion that Jack would still accept "what's right's right" and the dire reality as borne out in this scene. They recognize the symbolic meaning of the fact that Jack's painted anonymity is the last step of his almost complete metamorphosis into a black and green painted savage. The other savages swarming around Jack have undergone the same type of change; their irrational laughter should be commented on as an expression of their complete loss of moral values.

*Step 3:*
*Piggy's death*

Incorporating the students' answers to their homework question, Piggy's death is interpreted as the last link in a chain leading to the unleashing of despotic violence. Just as Simon's gospel went unheard in the storm, Piggy's essential message of civilization is refuted and knocked to pieces, a process symbolically accompanied by the shattering of the conch.
Student Paper No. 7 is presented, and puts Piggy's death in line with the other two deaths on the island, depicting the development from accidental loss of life (sheer negligence), via unintentional killing (blindness of frantic hysteria and ecstasy), to intentional murder. [Transparency], (cf. p. 118)
A discussion of the consequences of Piggy's death and the "possibilities of irresponsible authority" leads to a consideration of historical / political parallels.

*Step 4: (optional)*
*The development of Roger's character*

Chapter XI ends with a scene full of terrible implications: Roger advancing on Samneric with the "hangman's horror" and the threat of torture around him. Roger lends himself to a character analysis, as the passages referring to him are relatively short, and show revealing traits from the start. The "source of power" that starts pulsing in Roger before he kills Piggy is the same as welled up in him in Chapter IV when he started throwing stones at little Henry, but now it is stronger than the restraints that were holding him back then.
Student Paper No. 8 should be accompanied by a brief diagram (cf. p. 115).

*Step 5: (optional)*
*The development of the eight assemblies*

If a double period is available Student Paper No. 9 commends itself for presentation and discussion at this point, as a reconsideration of the boys' assemblies allows for a summing up of the major developments of the whole novel.

*Homework:*
Re-read Chapter XIIa–c. Prepare p. 204, 11 – p. 205,3 intensively.
Compare Ralph's encounter with the LoF with Simon's.

## Lesson 17: Defiance of Fatal Knowledge

### Didactic Considerations

The subject of Lesson 17 is Ralph's tragic dilemma, and his refusal to face and accept the nature of evil. Our attention in the first half of the final chapter is focused on Ralph, who is poised between a desperate attempt to cling to his reliance on "daylight sanity" and the realization of the horrors of darkness and death.
The course should discuss why Ralph, although haunted by the memory of Simon's and Piggy's deaths yet refuses to accept his "fatal knowledge". Does he refuse to face the logical conclusion that he is bound to be the next one to be killed after Simon and Piggy?
His encounter with the Lord of the Flies (XIIb) – an obvious parallel and contrast to Simon's – points in the same direction: significantly, the Lord of the Flies holds all the answers, but will not tell Ralph. Whereas Simon sought to understand, Ralph fights the recognition of evil.

The students should recognize and interpret Ralph's utter isolation and despair in XIIc, when the tragic paradox of his situation is epitomized in the line "Because I had some sense", (later on counterpoised by Eric's "Never mind what's sense. That's gone.")

### Plan of the Lesson

*Step 1:*
*Ambushing fears and defiance of fatal knowledge*

Both Steps 1 and 2 deal with the same theme: Ralph's defiance of his "fatal knowledge". Ralph's clearsighted realization of his state of affairs is contrasted with his refusal to accept this truth. It would indeed be fatal if Ralph really attempted to "rely on their common sense, their daylight sanity", as undoubtedly he would be killed by the savages.
While this part of the lesson can be dealt with fairly quickly, the next step is of great importance, as Ralph's failure to understand the message of the LoF can be interpreted as a further instance of his defiance of fatal knowledge.

*Step 2:*
*Ralph's encounter with the Lord of the Flies*

A quiet re-reading of this relatively short passage should precede the discussion.
The students compare Ralph's reaction to the LoF with Simon's.
Whilst Ralph quickly grasped the meaning of the conch as an instrument of civilized order in Chapter I, he now fails to understand the "message" of the LoF. The skull with the cynical grin holds Ralph's gaze like it did Simon's, but whereas Simon recognized and pene-

trated the nature of the evil that besets the boys, Ralph remains outside and feels that the skull "knows", but "won't tell" him the answers. His hitting out at the "filthy thing" that keeps bobbing back, grinning at him, shows that while Simon accepted the nature of evil, Ralph rejects it and remains ignorant.

*Step 3:*
*Ralph's tragic isolation*

The bitterness of Ralph's isolation also has a tragic touch about it. The class should define the paradox of Ralph's outcast state: the one who tried his best to do what he felt ought to be done, is now banned, damned, persecuted (and about to be executed!). The picture of Ralph kneeling "among the shadows" evokes the picture of Simon kneeling down with "the arrow of the sun" falling on him (p. 146, 24), suggesting that Simon was enlightened like a visionary or prophet, whilst Ralph remains blind (cf. p. 206, 15) because he refuses to see the fatal truth, even though the "striped inimical creatures" are constantly on his mind and the water below him "breathes" around the "death rock" reminding him of Piggy's fate.

*Homework:*
The students are to re-read Ch. XII d + e.

## Lesson 18: The Holocaust and the Rescue

### Didactic Considerations

The students are to sum up the main points of the last climactic happenings of the book as Ralph is tracked down and hunted like a wild animal: his hiding, his discovery, the various vicious attempts to kill him, his frenzied flight, his ultimate despair when down on his knees to receive the final stab ... Their attention is drawn to the fact that many of the images and motifs that were noted in the previous chapters blend and culminate in these scenes.

The greater part of the lesson, however, should be devoted to a discussion of Ralph's (and the other boys') "rescue" at the very end of the book. When the climax of the development on the island is reached, the timely arrival of the naval officer unexpectedly provides a turning point, and the perspectives of the event seem to change drastically – but do they really?

The officer's blatant ignorance in the face of the flames devouring the island must be questioned. Does he so blindly believe in the innocence of children that he fails to understand the message of the black clouds and the island's scorched earth?

Considering that memorable line towards the end of the novel ("Ralph wept for the end of innocence, the darkness of man's heart, and the fall through the air of the true, wise friend called Piggy.") the students will probably arrive at the conclusion that Ralph's weeping reveals the child as wiser than the adult: Ralph has gained the sort of insight that seems to be lacking in the officer. "It is Ralph who is 'grown-up', but he shows his adulthood by weeping. Golding needs him not only to see, but to register the proper response in pain and grief." (Kinkead-Weekes, p. 63).

## Plan of the Lesson

*Step 1:*
*The holocaust*

After an introductory question summarizing the way Ralph is hunted in Chapter XIId the students refer to their homework and list the seven stages of the hunt. Thus the relatively long passage of XIId can be covered without much loss of time. The class should note that many of the images and motifs recurring in the novel are brought together in this chapter; some examples should be analysed.
To mark the climax of Ralph's mad flight, the last part (p. 220, 8–34) should be read out.

*Step 2:*
*The rescue*

The main attention in this lesson ought to be directed towards the highly ambiguous "rescue" of the boys at the very end of the novel.
Again, time permitting, it would be good to have the students read the whole passage out (or at least p. 221).
The students note that the absolute climax of the book is at the same time its turning point, and they discuss this dramatic device (which Golding himself once called a "gimmick ending") and the change of perspectives that goes along with it. They note, too, that "rescue" is brought by a naval officer, a commander of a warship, which reminds the reader that the adult world still is – as it was at the beginning of the book – a world at war.
The final question aims at bringing the island microcosm into perspective with the macrocosm of the outer world. The end of Golding's book releases possibilities of further manifestations of the darkness of man's heart, a timeless, never-ending extension of the spiral of evil.

"The events witnessed in *LoF* do not end when the book does. If Roger's first stone leads to his murderous gesture, there is no reason why the rock thrown at Piggy should not also lead to the bomb launched against an enemy's country and ultimately to the atomic bomb that will destroy mankind. At this stage not only Ralph but the reader himself is aware that once the process has started there is no stopping the enraged monster." (J. Delbaere-Garant, p. 86).

*Homework:*
The two questions to be answered in writing (cf. Stundenblatt) are meant to provide material for a thorough final discussion of Golding's book.

## Lessons 19/20: The Parable of Man's Fall

### Didactic Considerations

As the book has now been read and discussed to the end, it is vital to make the students voice their personal reactions to *LoF*. How do they interpret the meaning of the end? What do they make of the whole story? Is there some sort of a message in Golding's novel, and if so which? What effect did the novel have on them personally? Can they think of comparisons with other books they have read?
These final discussions should allow the class a great deal of leeway to give them ample opportunity to formulate their own response to the book and to express their

individual thoughts and ideas. The teacher should therefore only provide the framework of the last two lessons with his thematic focal points. (It would be good to have a double period available.)
Only after the students have voiced their opinion about the meaning of the end of *LoF* is it feasible to present the text below, which contains Golding's own comment on the intention of his novel. "The overall picture was to be the tragic lesson that . . . the only enemy of man is inside him." (Hot Gates, p. 89).
As Golding himself acknowledges his indebtedness to R. M. Ballantyne's *The Coral Island,* which he uses as a counterfoil (cf. p. 102 and 122), the logical next step would be to consider the essential differences between Ballantyne's book and *LoF*. Likewise D. Defoe's *Robinson Crusoe* could be referred to and – in its essentials – be compared with *LoF*, as Christian optimism and faith play a central part in *Robinson Crusoe* as it does in *The Coral Island*, whereas the Bible and Christian dogma are never even mentioned in *LoF*. To ensure valuable contributions from the students in the analysis of the theme of *LoF,* those students who previously presented their papers on *The Coral Island* and *Robinson Crusoe* should be called on to state obvious differences they noticed between *LoF* and the other island adventure books. Likewise, when the discussion touches on the question of the essential nature of man, the student who studied the text on Thomas Hobbes' *Leviathan* (cf. p. 125) could contribute quotations to animate the controversy.

**W. Golding on the Nature of Man**

Before the second world war I believed in the perfectibility of social man; that a correct structure of society would produce goodwill; and that therefore you could remove all social ills by a reorganization of society. It is possible that today I believe something of the same again; but after the war I did not because I was unable to. I had discovered what one man could do to another. I am not talking of one man killing another with a gun, or dropping a bomb on him or blowing him up or torpedoing him. I am thinking of the vileness beyond all words that went on, year after year, in the totalitarian states. It is bad enough to say that so many Jews were exterminated in this way and that, (. . .) but there were things done during that period from which I still have to avert my mind lest I should be physically sick. They were not done by the headhunters of New Guinea, or by some primitive tribe in the Amazon. They were done, skilfully, coldly, by educated men, doctors, lawyers, by men with a tradition of civilization behind them, to beings of their own kind . . .
It seemed to me that man's capacity for greed, his innate cruelty and selfishness was being hidden behind a kind of pair of political pants. I believed then that man was sick – not exceptional man, but average man. I believed that the condition of man was to be a morally diseased creation and that the best job I could do at the time, was to trace the connection between his diseased nature and the international mess he gets himself into. . . .
Man is a fallen being. He is gripped by original sin. His nature is sinful and his state perilous. . . .

I looked round me for some convenient form in which this thesis might be worked out, and found it in the play of children. I was well situated for this, since at this time I was teaching them. Moreover, I am a son, brother, and father. I have lived for many years with small boys, and understand and know them with awful precision. I decided to take the literary convention of boys on an island, only make them real boys instead of paper cutouts with no life in them; and try to show how the shape of the society they evolved would be conditioned by their diseased, their fallen nature.

It is worth looking for a moment at the great original of boys on an island. This is *The Coral Island,* published a century ago, at the height of Victorian smugness, ignorance, and prosperity.

Ballantyne's island was a nineteenth-century island inhabited by English boys; mine was to be a twentieth-century island inhabited by English boys. . . .

My book was to say: you think that now the war is over and an evil thing destroyed, you are safe because you are naturally kind and decent. But I know why the thing rose in Germany. I know it could happen in any country. It could happen here.

So the boys try to construct a civilization on the island; but it breaks down in blood and terror because the boys are suffering from the terrible disease of being human.

The overall picture was to be the tragic lesson . . . that the only enemy of man is inside him.

From: *William Golding, Fable,* in: The Hot Gates, Faber and Faber, London 1965, p. 86–89

**Annotations:**

*vileness* shameful and disgusting behaviour – *a pair of political pants* a political mask, taboo – *perilous* dangerous – *smugness* self-satisfaction

In addition the texts on theories of innate aggression (cf. p. 105 f.) might be presented, which would add a further (psychoanalytical and ethological) dimensions, and could lead to a discussion of the reason for atrocities in war, and ultimately to the principal question of the origin of wars (cf. Additional Lesson).

Depending on how much time is left after the finalizing discussion of the "message" of *LoF*, Golding's literary technique of presenting his story (although touched upon on various occasions in the course of the analysis) could be summed up systematically to heighten the students' awareness of, and their attention to, the elements that contribute to the overall fabric of *LoF.* Better still, an additional lesson should be dedicated to an analysis of the structural elements in *LoF,* especially on repetition and contrast as a stylistic means.

## Plan of the Lesson

### *Step 1: Rescue or salvation?*

As, despite Ralph's rescue, the end of Golding's book offers no tangible solution, the students are invited to state what

meaning the final episode of *LoF* conveys to them individually. This discussion then leads logically on to the analysis of the main theme of the book.
(As an option, a brief review of the development of *LoF* from the beginning to the end could be included (cf. BD Stundenblatt S. 41), indicating the vicious circle that takes the boys back to their original point of departure.)

*Step 2:*
*Analysis of the theme of LoF*

This phase of the lesson should be handled almost entirely by the students themselves. After a "brainstorming" opening question to the whole class (the answer to which could be jotted down on one side of the board leaving room on the right side for later analysis) the ensuing discussion should be supported and channelled by Golding's own comment on the intention of his novel (cf. p. 101f.) and by three to-the-point student contributions. The students who previously presented papers on Defoe's *Robinson Crusoe* and Ballantyne's *Coral Island* (cf. p. 101) are now asked to make brief statements on some essential differences between those books and *LoF*. Another student supplements these statements with a brief outline of the main idea of Hobbes' *Leviathan* to put Golding's *LoF* into yet another perspective. Two Hobbes' quotes could be displayed on an overhead projector. (In this connection the students should remember, and refer to p. 115 in *LoF* where Golding himself makes metaphorical use of the word 'leviathan'.)
After that the course is asked to try and focus Golding's main concern on one central point (→ man's "fall"). The analysis of instances and further illustrations of the boys' "fall" could take place in group work, or in pairs, to save time. The findings are discussed by the whole group. The recognition of some universal aspects implied by the author rounds this part of the lesson off.
(As the teacher may not want to deal with all of the five points listed under Step 2 on the Stundenblatt, a selection commends itself.)

*Step 3:*
*The message of LoF*

The two questions to be dealt with as homework from Lesson 18 are the basis for a strongly student-oriented final analysis. One or two students read out their answers to each question and the group subsequently respond with comments and further opinions. On one side of the board the teacher writes down the main points made by the students.

*Homework:*
The homework assignment depends on whether or not the additional lessons as subsequently suggested are included.
- Homework for an additional lesson on the theory of innate aggressiveness: Read and prepare the text on "Innate Aggressiveness". Sum up the two positions presented.
- Homework for an additional lesson on structural elements in Golding's *LoF*: Select two passages from *LoF* which you consider well-written, and try to explain how Golding achieves this effect.

## Additional Lesson: The Theory of Innate Aggressiveness

The reading and preparation of the text on p. 105f. on the proponents and critics of the psychoanalytical and ethological theories of "innate aggressiveness" is intended to widen the scope of the analysis of the "message" of *LoF*. The brief summary of theories of aggression from T. Hobbes to Konrad Lorenz, and the two positions stated, should be discussed. The phrase "letting loose the beast", and the cue of the massacre at MyLai in Vietnam, will lead the students to consider cruelty and atrocities in wars, and might spark off discussions on parallels with the development of evil in Hitler Germany.

*Points for Discussion:*

- What are the two positions presented in the article?

- The instinct theory (man is aggressive by nature) as proposed by Hobbes, James, McDougall, Freud, and Konrad Lorenz claims that man's innate instincts of pugnacity, anger, and resentment, of cruelty and the desire to hurt are the cause of wars. The behaviourists (Lorenz) consider the aggression drive inherited. The critics of this theory claim that the instinct theory is unscientific, too metaphysical and mystic. The natural sciences have not yet discovered any genetic data that would explain hereditary transmission of aggressiveness.

- Do you accept the instinct theory as propagated by the psychoanalytic and the behaviourist schools (S. Freud and K. Lorenz) or would you side with their critics?

- Compare the journalist's phrase "Letting loose the beast" (referring to Vietnam massacres) with the "beast" in *LoF*.

- In both instances the "beast" is seen as something inside the human being that is liberated as a destructive force. The "beast" comes out in many guises; especially gruesome in wartime cruelties such as the MyLai massacre, or the holocaust of the mass killing of Jews in World War II.

- Are you convinced by S. Freud's belief that instinctual impulses will be restricted by cultural evolution?
  - The political and historical developments of the 20th century have not really proved Freud right. On the other hand, our cultural, social, and moral conscience should be a safeguard against our propensity for aggression.
- What, in your opinion, can be done to prevent developments that lead to bestial conflicts and wars?
  - Application of reason and common sense, propagation of and adamant adherence to ethical values, development of a cultural conscience, strengthening of the peace movement in its many facets, critical self-awareness.

**Innate Aggressiveness**

Instinct theory is perhaps the most Hobbesian of the theories of human behavior which attempt to explain aggression. This theory, which holds that man is by nature aggressive, has many illustrious proponents. William James (1890) states that the human race was reared in a "gory cradle" and its members are the lineal representatives of successful enactors of slaughter and carnage. Thus, the instincts of pugnacity, anger, and resentment smolder within humans ready at any moment to erupt. Mc Dougall (1908) also argues that man possessed, among many other instincts, an instinct for pugnacity. Freud (1922) states that cruelty and a desire to hurt others deliberately is a prominent feature of the human psyche. He attributes this desire to the death instinct. ...

Powered by the libido, this drive, according to Freud, is the cause of war and a cause for pessimism insofar as man's future is concerned. In a letter to Albert Einstein in 1932 concerning war, Freud argued against the feasibility of ridding man of his aggressive instincts. The diversion of aggressive impulses so that they are expressed in other forms than war would be enough of an accomplishment. Although Freud was concerned about time running out, cultural evolution, he believed, is the means by which instinctual impulses will be restricted and displaced. In the main, the belief in man's innate aggressiveness is a common feature shared by those in the psychoanalytic school.

Those ethologists who extrapolate the results of their studies of lower animals to humans also tend to view man as an innately aggressive animal. In this sense, ethological theories of human aggression parallel in biological science the philosophy of Thomas Hobbes. For example, Lorenz (1966) argues that homo sapiens is even more aggressive than other animals because of his propensity for aggression. ...

Aphoristically, Lorenz states that man has "... in his hand the atom bomb, the product of his intelligence, in his heart the aggression drive inherited from his anthropoid ancestors, which this same intelligence cannot control ..."

**Annotations:**
*innate* in one's nature – *proponent* s. o. who proposes sth. – *to state* to express in words – *to rear* to bring up – *gory:* bloody – *enactor* performer, executor – *carnage* killing – *pugnacity* willingness to fight – *to smolder* to burn slowly without flame; *here* lie waiting – *deliberately* on purpose – *drive* dt. Trieb – *feasibility* possibility – *to rid s.o. of sth.* to free s.o. of sth. – *ethology* the study of animal behaviour – *propensity* natural tendency

## A Critique of the Theory of Innate Aggressiveness

Ethological theory has not gone unchallenged. The works, in particular, of Lorenz (1966), and Morris (1967) have been widely criticized. The concept of instinct applied to man whether used by the Freudians or the ethologists is unproductive scientifically because it explains nothing. To label aggressiveness as "human nature" connotes immutability, and behavior so classified is placed beyond the limits of scientific investigation. ...

Furthermore, the concept of instinct, which is employed to explain human aggression, takes on a metaphysical quality comparable to notions of vital forces such as entelechy, a notion of the ancient Greeks, or Bergson's (1911) *élan vital.* Indeed, Montagu (1968) likens these descriptions of man's innate aggression to the concept of original sin and innate depravity. (It is interesting to note in this respect that the title of Lorenz' book in its original German is *Das Sogenannte Böse* – the so-called evil.)

An example of how this Hobbesian notion of innate bestiality has influenced the thinking of even an enlightened journalist is illustrated in an article by the editorialist Tom Wicker (1969) on the apparent massacre at My Lai. In a section entitled "Letting Loose the Beast," Wicker says, "My Lai in fact proves nothing specific about Vietnam; it only shows once again what man is capable of once he lets loose the beast within himself". ...

There are as yet no convincing genetic data – ... to explain the hereditary transmission of the ... amount of aggressive instinct in human beings.

From: *Lefkowitz/Eron/Walder/Huesmann, Growing Up to be Violent: A Study of the Development of Aggression,* Pergamon Press, New York, 1977, p. 8ff.

**Annotations:**
*to connote* to imply – *immutability* impossibility of change – *entelechy* moving towards potential perfection – *depravity* corruptness

## Additional Lesson: Structural Elements in Golding's "LoF"

In the course of our analysis of Golding's *LoF* we have frequently noticed a network of interrelated verbal and pictorial references, which shows how much care and artistic skill has gone into the construction of the novel. It is well worthwhile studying the technique and the style of *LoF* in a separate lesson.
The students should be asked to refer to the passages they selected as "well written" (= assignment), and to give reasons for their choice. This leads to determining some of the elements that contribute to the overall effect of *LoF*. Four such elements might be listed (if necessary with some help from the teacher):

- plot and language
- the author's point of view
- imagery and symbolism
- repetition and contrast

Two alternatives lend themselves to classroom analysis:

*a) Structural Elements in LoF*
The teacher may decide to have the class examine all of the four elements listed above (in pairs, or in four groups, respectively). As completeness is not aimed at, ten minutes should suffice to gather enough examples to be subsequently presented by the individual groups, and noted down on the board or transparency (cf. p. 108).

*b) Repetition and Contrast as Stylistic Means in LoF*
Special emphasis could be laid on the predominant stylistic means employed by the author, repetition (or parallelism) and contrast with regard both to actual occurences (such as the meetings, games, expeditions, etc.) and to the imagery and symbolism used throughout.
To get the students started, the text "Rhythm and Expansion in *LoF*" (cf. p. 109f.) could be presented, perused quietly and read out by a student. The class would list some examples of contrastive and repetitive patterns mentioned in the text of the worksheet, and could then complement them with further examples in which the pattern of repetition and contrast becomes apparent.
As Student Papers No. 10 and No. 6 offer good examples of repetition and contrast, at least one of them should be included in the lesson. If Student Paper No. 10 is read out in class, No. 6 might be presented in a transparency survey (cf. p. 114f., for example)

### Possible Questions and Stimuli

*a) Structural Elements in LoF*

- What elements can we determine that contribute to the total effect of this novel?
- How would you characterize the development of the plot in *LoF*?
- Comment on the author's point of view in *LoF*.

- Do you agree with the opinion stated by many critics of *LoF* that Golding's language is "simple" and "straightforward"?
- Give examples of imagery and symbolism in *LoF*. (List them in contrasting pairs whenever possible.) BD / Transparency
- List examples of repetitions and contrasts in *LoF*. BD / Transparency

*b) Repetition and Contrast as Stylistic Means in LoF*

- What elements can we determine that contribute to the total effect of this novel?
- Text "Rhythm and Expansion in *LoF*"
  quiet reading → text is read out
- What contrasts are mentioned in the text?
- Can you add to the list?
- What does Golding seem to suggest by introducing correspondences between setting and characters?
- Student Paper No. 10 "Stone Throwing and Rock Rolling in *LoF*"
  is read out and discussed
- Student Paper No. 6 "The Four Expeditions"
  a transparency is displayed with a survey of the development
- Summing up:
  What effect does Golding achieve by having this pattern of repetition and contrast permeate the whole novel?

**Board diagram:**

**Structural elements in Golding's "LoF"**

*Plot and Language*

| | |
|---|---|
| straightforward narration | apparent simplicity of language |
| progressive development of plot | dialogues: schoolboy parley |
| clear chain of events | descriptive text: often endowed with unusual words, sometimes ornate |
| only two (three) short flashbacks | |

*Author's Point of View*

| | |
|---|---|
| – mostly: third person narrator : | objective distance |
| – sometimes entering a character's mind ("omniscient author") : | subjective, relativating |

*Imagery and Symbolism*

e. g.: the island boat ("moving steadily astern")
the assembly boat (triangle), apex → darkness
the pig's head, etc.

| | | | | | |
|---|---|---|---|---|---|
| mountain top | ↔ | jungle | parliamentary triangle | ↔ | tribal circle |
| palm trees | ↔ | creepers | scent of flowers | ↔ | smell of droppings |
| fruit trees | ↔ | dead trees | fruit diet | ↔ | pig meat |
| saplings | ↔ | skull-like coconuts | shelters | ↔ | caves |
| butterflies | ↔ | flies | home-building | ↔ | hunting |
| fire | ↔ | ashes | Piggy's glasses | ↔ | Jack's knife |
| conch | ↔ | pig's head | "friendly side" of island | ↔ | "unfriendly" side |

*Repetition and Contrast*

the meetings
the "games"
the "expeditions"

the fires
the rituals
the killings, etc.

**Rhythm and Expansion in *Lord of the Flies***

Water and rocks, ebb and flow, angles and circles, microcosm and macrocosm, reason and intuition, good and evil, flies and butterflies: rhythm beats in *Lord of the Flies,* sometimes loud, sometimes with "an undertone less perceptible than the susurration of the blood," but always with the regularity of waves against the reef. This continual back-and-forth motion, the rhythm of life, is complemented by a rhythmic use of gradation suggesting the constant progress of evil. The killing of pigs and the throwing of rocks, two important activities of the boys on the island, provide a metaphorical structure for the illustration of the author's theme.

In the description of the setting is a basic opposition between sea and island, liquidity and hardness, flux and fixity, roundness and angularity. The "circular horizon of water" contains the "square motif of the landscape."

Sea and sky, islands and stars answer each other: the sky mirrors itself in the water together with the "angular bright constellations". At a mile's distance from the island and parallel to it lies a coral reef, against which waves break so that the beach is duplicated in the sea, "as though a giant had bent down to reproduce the shape of the island in a flowing chalk line but tired before he had finished." Finally, there is a reminder of the water motif in the island, reminder of the rock motif in the sea. As in the yin and yang of the Chinese, there is a black patch in the white surface and a white patch in the black, a piece of squareness in the liquid element and a pool in the island.

There is rhythm also in the abrupt succession of night and day and even in the configuration of the island itself.

"The first rhythm that they became used to was the slow swing from dawn to quick dusk". Time is no longer measured by the clock but by the regular movement of sunlight from the horizontal at dawn to the perpendicular at noon and back to the horizontal in the evening. On the island the sandy beach is interrupted by the "square motif" of the mountain: "The most usual feature of the rock was a pink cliff surmounted by a skewed block; and that again surmounted, and that again, till the pinkness became a stack of balanced rock projecting through the looped fantasy of the forest creepers". As this rhythmical alternation of vertical and horizontal planes measures the tropical day and underlies the structure of the island, so contrastive and repetitive patterns govern the structure of the novel, which is built on a contrapuntal balance of opposites and on repetitions, echoes, parallels, which blend and culminate in the last chapter.

From the beginning we are aware of correspondences: a bird's cry on the first page is answered by Piggy's voice, and the noise emitted by Ralph's blowing of the conch is echoed by the mountain. Even the fundamental patterns of the geophysical world will be unconsciously imitated by the boys in their activities: the contrast between the circular horizon of the sea and the angular shape of the island is reproduced in the circles and triangles into which they fall when they come together. When they hold meetings the boys form a triangle which eventually deteriorates into a sketchy and empty shape. When they hunt, Jack's choir-boys form a circle around the pig, and this pattern becomes neater as the boys revert to savagery.

By introducing correspondences between setting and characters Golding intimates that the same law governs the geophysical world and the world of man. Human nature is an aspect of nature at large.

After making clear, through a rhythmical balance of opposites recalling the waves of the ocean, that all things, animate and inanimate, are governed by the same law, that evil does not spare man any more than it does nature, that each living creature is in turn hunter and hunted, Golding shows, through a series of repetitions expanding like the movement of the tides, that there is no stopping evil.

Abridged from: *Jeanne Delbaere-Garant, Rhythm and Expansion in "LoF"*, in Biles/Evans, William Golding, Some Critical Considerations, Kentucky U.P., 1978, pp. 72–86

**Annotations:**

*susurration* running noise – *gradation* gradual change – *skewed* turned to one side – *to intimate* to show clearly – *to spare s. o.* to refrain from damaging

## Student Papers

1 Report on Daniel Defoe's *Robinson Crusoe*. Comment in a few sentences on what strikes you as notably different from Golding's novel as far as you can see at this point. (The student may make use of text on p. 120)

2 Report on R. M. Ballantyne's *The Coral Island* and compare plot and characters with Golding's *Lord of the Flies*. (The student may make use of the information given in the texts on p. 122ff.)

3 Trace the development of rational action versus irrational action in Chapters I to VI.

4 Give a brief report on Thomas Hobbes' political/philosophical treatise *The Leviathan* Part I, Chapter XI. (The student may make use of the information given in the text on p. 125)

5 Examine the symbolism of the island geography.
- Describe the two opposite sides of the island and interpret their symbolic meanings.
- Describe the two corresponding seascapes on either side, and comment.
- Interpret the symbolic meaning of some special features of the island, such as the mountain top, the platform, the jungle, the forest, the fruit trees, Castle Rock, etc.

6 Compare the four expeditions on the island.
- What is the purpose of each expedition and who participates in them?
- Characterize the mood of each expedition and comment on the development that takes place in the boys.

7 Compare the three deaths of boys on the island.
Why does the boy with the mulberry mark die, what is the reason for Simon's death, and why does Piggy die?
(Comment also on the description of Simon's and of Piggy's deaths and on the way their dead bodies are taken away by the sea.)

8 Trace, and comment on, the development of Roger's character.

9 Describe the eight assemblies and show how the boys' meetings reflect the gradual deterioration of the civilized element.
- Note the change in Ralph's manner of thinking and speaking at these meetings.
- Note the changes in the description of the meeting places.
- Note the significance of the conch in the meetings.

10 Describe Golding's technique of depicting the progress of evil by following up the throwing of stones and the rolling of rocks in the novel.
- Where do the boys first come across rocks and how do they respond?
- Comment on the scene in Chapter IV in which Percival has sand thrown in his eyes (first by Maurice, then by Johnny!)
- Why and how does Roger throw stones at Henry? What is Henry's reaction?
- What are the further steps in the development of stone-throwing and rock-rolling?

---

## Material and/or Expected Results for Student Papers

*Student Paper No. 3:*
*The development of rational action versus irrational action in Chapters I to VI*

| rational | irrational |
|---|---|
| – using conch as signal horn and as giving the right to speak | – forgetting and disregarding the conch |
| – having assemblies to determine their actions | – breaking assemblies up |
| – agreeing on rules | – disobeying the rules |
| – going on expeditions to explore the island | – rolling rocks downhill, smashing scars into forest |
| – keeping a signal fire going | – neglecting the fire, accidentally killing a little boy |
| – having hunters to get meat | – Jack's compulsion to hunt and kill |
| – building shelters | – destroying sandcastles, throwing sand and stones, rolling rocks |
| – providing a supply of water | – neglecting their duties |
| – using certain rocks as "lavatories" | – befouling the place everywhere |
| | – developing fear of the dark, "snake things", "beastie", "ghosts", "the beast" |
| | – dancing, chanting, etc. |

*Student Paper No. 5*
*The symbolism of the island geography*

The two sides of the island, the "friendly" side (with the forest, the beach, the pool, and the platform) and the "unfriendly" side (with the dangerous rocks and the "gullies") are symbolic of the human potential: the restrained, controlled, democratic, "good" side, and the anarchic, unrestrained, "evil" side in man. So are the two corresponding seascapes: the calm lagoon, sheltered, beautiful, peaceful; and the wild swell of the ocean on the side of the monstrous "sleeping leviathan".

Some examples of possible interpretations of the island geography:

| | |
|---|---|
| The mountain top: | hope, vision, recognition of truth |
| The scar: | vulneration of nature through the intrusion of human aggression |
| The platform: | reason, order, stability, common sense |
| The forest: | darkness of the human spirit, fear |
| The jungle: | the fearful, intricate maze of the world, containing beauty ("candle bushes", butterflies) as well as danger ("the beast") |
| The fruit trees: | fertility, paradisiac abundance |
| The palm trees: | shelter, fertility, protection |
| Castle Rock: | barrenness, infertility, threat |
| The caves: | primitive existence |
| White sand: | infertility, death |
| Stones, rocks: | violence, danger, aggressiveness |
| Creepers: | hindrance to progress, restriction |

*Student Paper No. 6:*
*Comparison of the four expeditions on the island*

| | | | | |
|---|---|---|---|---|
| EXPEDITION NO. 1 | (p. 25–34) to the top of the mountain | | | |
| PURPOSE: | to explore the place to make sure it is an island | | | |
| PARTICIPANTS: | RALPH | JACK | SIMON | |
| | wants to draw a map | wants to kill a pig | sees "candle-buds" in bushes | |
| | common sense | action | imagination | |
| MOOD: | Excitement with the glamour of the island paradise; the boys are united in the joy of common discovery and experience. | | | |
| EXPEDITION NO. 2 | (2a: p. 112–119) to the other end of the island<br>(2b: p. 127–136) to the top of the mountain | | | |
| PURPOSE: | to look for the beast | | | |
| PARTICIPANTS: 2a: | RALPH | JACK | SIMON | ROGER |
| | common sense | hunting compulsion, tactics | sympathetic, understanding | sombre gloom |
| 2b: | RALPH | JACK | – | ROGER |
| MOOD: | Rising antagonism between Ralph and Jack. | | | |

| | | | |
|---|---|---|---|
| EXPEDITION NO. 3 | (p. 178, p. 183–186) to Ralph's and Piggy's shelter | | |
| PURPOSE: | to steal Piggy's glasses (after Jack has formed his own group) | | |
| PARTICIPANTS: | JACK<br>irrational<br>evil violence | ROGER<br>dark, sinister<br>brute force | MAURICE<br>dto. |
| MOOD: | Dark hatred. The constructive aim degenerates into robbery and destruction. | | |
| EXPEDITION NO. 4 | (p. 208–220) all over the island | | |
| PURPOSE: | to hunt Ralph down and kill him like a pig | | |
| PARTICIPANTS: | JACK and his whole tribe | | |
| MOOD: | Irrational savage ecstasy; liberation of evil destructive forces | | |

*Student Paper No. 8:*
*Roger's development*

| | | | | | | | |
|---|---|---|---|---|---|---|---|
| Roger is slight, furtive, introverted | throws stones at a littlun, teasing(?), aiming to miss, conditioned by civilization | takes part in hunters' game, tries to hurt Robert | torments a sow in a cruel and very brutal way | Roger admires his chief and irresponsible authority | throws stones aiming to miss, feels his own power | kills Piggy with a rock | becomes the torturer |
| p. 23 | p. 65–67 | p. 126 | p. 149–150 | p. 176 | p. 199 | p. 200 | p. 201 |

*Student Paper No. 9:*
*The eight assemblies*

| ASSEMBLY | TIME AND PURPOSE | RALPH | MEETING PLACE | CONCH |
|---|---|---|---|---|
| No. 1 (p. 18ff) | After Ralph's blowing the conch, Ralph is elected chief. Decision to explore the island. | Needs time to think, but is determined, self-confident, optimistic | The platform, ordered grouping. | Delicate, creamy, "powerful", respected, "trumpet-thing". |
| No. 2 (p. 35–42) | After the first expedition. Decision to light a fire. | Talks fluently now, can explain his thoughts, disregards interruptions, repeats sentences for emphasis, is flustered by irrational beast-story, firmly establishes his chieftaincy. | The platform (parliamentary triangle). ↓ | "Cream and pink shell", symbol of order, cradled and cherished by Piggy, disregarded by Jack. |
| (p. 46–51) | Decision to have more rules. | | The mountain top. | Jack: "doesn't count on the mountain". |
| No. 3 (p. 83–100) | After the fire has gone out. Ralph wants to "put things straight". | Finds it difficult to think concentratedly; new mood of comprehension, realizes dirt and decay, adjusts his values. | "Irregular and sketchy" platform triangle, apex towards dark jungle, "ill-balanced twister", dead tree. | Ralph feels "affectionate reverence" for the conch. |
| No. 4 (p. 109) | After Samneric's report of the beast. Decision to search for the beast. | Quiet, scared, but maintaining his chieftaincy despite Jack's interruptions. | The platform triangle. | Ralph holds conch up! Jack: "we don't need the conch any more". |

| | | | | |
|---|---|---|---|---|
| No. 5 (p. 138–143) | Called by Jack after the second expedition to challenge Ralph's leadership.<br>Decision to build a fire on the beach. | Silent, depressed, bites his fingernails. | The platform triangle. | "Inexpertly" blown by Jack, then laid down and deserted. |
| No. 6 (p. 156–157) | After Jack's raid of the fire. Need for ritual! | Holds a lame speech. A "shutter" flicks in his brain; he is "puzzled", helpless, pessimistic. | The platform. (more and more deserted). | "White" now, loses in importance. |
| No. 7 (p. 187–190) | After Piggy's glasses have been stolen.<br>Decision to ask for Piggy's glasses back. | Speaks with pauses, a "curtain" flickers in his brain again, he becomes silent, insecure, helpless, frustrated. | The almost completely deserted platform. | "Fragile and white", is carried along by Piggy, "against all odds". |
| No. 8 (p. 193–201) | Ralph tries, unsuccessfully, to call an assembly at the Castle Rock neck. | Becomes angry, furious, screams, fights, is injured, runs for his life. | Outside Castle Rock. | Explodes and ceases to exist. |

*Student Paper No. 7:*
*The three deaths on the island*

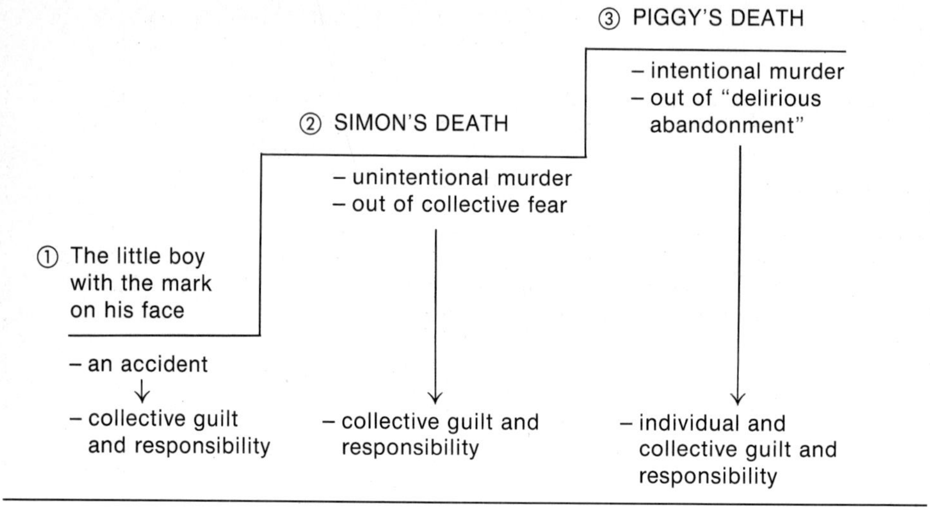

*Student Paper No. 10:*
*The throwing of stones and the rolling of rocks*

| | | The boys' response: | Consequences: | Implications: |
|---|---|---|---|---|
| p. 29: | Jack, Ralph, Simon push a rock large as a motor car into the sea | "challenge"<br>"triumph" | smashing a hole into forest/ "enraged monster", "like a bomb" | a game!- |
| p. 65: | Roger and Maurice destroy sandcastles, scatter stones, get sand into Percival's eyes | Roger & Maurice feel the "unease of wrongdoing" / form "outlines of an excuse" | Percival cries | destructive behaviour |
| | little Johnny throws sand into Percival's eyes | (= imitation of Roger and Maurice) | Percival cries | a game, in childish imitation |
| | Roger throws stones at Henry | "aiming to miss" (taboo of old life) | Henry laughs (does not understand) | game no more! (Roger's eyelids flutter, he breathes quickly!) |
| p. 116: | Jack: "if an enemy came ... one heave and ..." | "exulting" | rock would kill | war-game |
| p. 118: | Roger & others push a big rock into the sea | "off their rockers" | thunderous spray leaps up | destructive game |
| p. 176: | Robert leans on lever under rock | (admired by Roger!) | rock would thunder down to the neck | meant to kill Ralph & Piggy |
| p. 194: | Roger throws stones | "aiming to miss" | Sam almost slips | |
| 199: | Roger throws stones | obeying "some source of power" | | |
| 200: | Roger sends rock down | | Piggy is killed | |
| p. 213: | Jack's tribe send huge rocks down on Ralph | intent on killing | | games have turned into murderous reality! |

*Student Paper No. 1:*
*Daniel Defoe's Robinson Crusoe*

**Daniel Defoe, Robinson Crusoe**

This new type of Englishman, empirical, self-reliant, energetic, and with the sense of a direct relation with a God made in his own image, Daniel Defoe expresses in the character of Crusoe. ...

The secret of the uncanny verisimilitude he achieves has often been analysed. He was the master of the literal; he produces his illusion of complete reality by employing a mass of circumstantial detail of a kind no one, we think as we read, would bother to invent. In *Robinson Crusoe,* the shipwreck and the hero's sojourn on his island, though the most important parts of the book, are still only parts. Before he reaches the point of being cast away, Crusoe passes through a whole gamut of adventures, including a period in slavery to the Barbary corsairs. By the time we reach the shipwreck it has already become in our mind something that would inevitably happen to a man like him: it is, in other words, in character. The smaller lies have conditioned us to accept the bigger one. It is certainly incredible enough: Crusoe is on his island twenty-eight years, two months, and nineteen days. The exactitude is characteristic; it is partly because we can follow Crusoe's experiences at times from day to day and always from year to year, with the dates given, that we swallow the impossible. But we accept Crusoe's story even more readily because Defoe puts the stress all the time not on the island or on the dangers surrounding his hero but on Crusoe the man himself. It is Crusoe who fills the picture, and he does so as a truly heroic figure, a man dominating nature. Crusoe is the first great individualist, but he convinces as such by his ordinariness.

As Coleridge points out, in what he does Crusoe 'arrives at no excellence ... the carpentering, tailoring, pottery, etc., are all just what will answer his purpose ... Crusoe rises only to the point to which all men may be made to feel that they might.'

It was Coleridge's contention that Crusoe was 'the universal representative, the person, for whom every reader could substitute himself'.

But there is also the other side to Crusoe, the religious side, his preoccupation with theology, his moralizing.

Crusoe is God's Englishman, and God helps those who help themselves. The sense of partnership between God and man is with Crusoe all the time.

The two sides of Crusoe, the practical and the religious, come together in such a passage, which Coleridge acclaimed as 'worthy of Shakespeare', as:

"I smil'd to myself at the sight of this money: 'O drug!' said I aloud. ... However, upon second thoughts, I took it away; and wrapping all this in a piece of canvas. ..."

No doubt Defoe began with no other intention than to write a fake-autobiography of a sailor like Selkirk, but the reader who returns to it to-day as an adult cannot fail to see in it more than the adventures of the castaway on an uninhabited island. Indeed, simply by describing those adventures Defoe had done more: he had dramatized as sharply as possible the inescapable solitariness of each man in his relation to God and the universe, and it is the index of his triumph with his hero that Crusoe still remains adequate as a representation of the human being in this timeless situation.

From: *Walter Allen, The English Novel,* Penguin Books, Harmondsworth, 1958, p. 38 ff.

**Annotations**
*self-reliant* having confidence in one's powers – *uncanny* strange – *verisimilitude* appearance of truth – *sojourn* stay – *gamut* range – *inevitable* sure to happen – *contention* here: conviction – *solitariness:* loneliness

**Ballantyne's The Coral Island**

I can do no better than quote to you Professor Carl Niemeyer's sketch of this book.

'Ballantyne shipwrecks his three boys – Jack, eighteen; Ralph, the narrator, aged fifteen; and Peterkin Gay, a comic sort of boy, aged thirteen – somewhere in the South Seas on an uninhabited coral island. Jack is a natural leader, but both Ralph and Peterkin have abilities valuable for survival. Jack has the most common sense and foresight, but Peterkin turns out to be a skilful killer of pigs and Ralph, when later in the book he is separated from his friends and alone on a schooner, coolly navigates back to Coral Island by dead reckoning, a feat sufficiently impressive. The boys' life on the island is idyllic; and they are themselves without malice or wickedness, tho' there are a few curious episodes in which Ballantyne seems to hint at something he himself understands as little as do his characters. ... Ballantyne's book raises the problem of evil – which comes to the boys not from within themselves but from the outside world. Tropical nature to be sure, is kind, but the men of this non-Christian world are bad. For example the island is visited by savage cannibals, one canoeful pursuing another, who fight a cruel and bloody battle observed by the horrified boys, and then go away. A little later, the island is again visited, this time by pirates (i. e. white men who have renounced or scorned their Christian heritage) who succeed in capturing Ralph. In due time the pirates are deservedly destroyed, and in the final episode of the book the natives undergo an unmotivated conversion to Christianity, which effects a total change in their nature just in time to rescue the boys from their clutches. Thus Ballantyne's view of man is seen to be optimistic, like his view of English boys' pluck and resourcefulness, which subdues tropical islands as triumphantly as England imposes empire and religion on lawless breeds of men.'

From: *William Golding, Fable,* in: The Hot Gates, Faber and Faber, London 1965, p. 88/89

**Annotations**

*feat* a difficult task well done – *malice* ill will – *to renounce* to give up – *to scorn* to feel contempt for – *clutches* here: fangs, power – *pluck* courage – *resourcefulness* here: quick wit

**R. M. Ballantyne, The Coral Island**

The story of *The Coral Island* is told in the first person by the hero Ralph (equivalent to the Ralph of *Lord of the Flies,* whose surname is never given), a boy of fifteen who has always had a passion to go to sea. His two companions on a voyage to the South Seas are Jack Martin, 'a tall, strapping, broad-shouldered youth of eighteen' and Peterkin Gay, a boy of fourteen who is 'little, quick, funny, decidedly mischievous'. These two approximate in the loosest way to Jack and Simon in *Lord of the Flies.* The boys are shipwrecked on a coral island, and immediately start to fend for themselves. They have many adventures, and live for a time on the tropical fruit and vegetables available, as well as fish and oysters. They soon discover traces of man and of animals, but their first major encounter is with a shark. After this, Jack persuades the others to explore the whole island, one of his reasons being that their need is to find some animal food.

They make bows and arrows and clubs, spears and slings. They find some pigs, but these get away, though Peterkin, who has gone off on his own, has succeeded in spearing a piglet. They have their first real feast on this, a vegetable called the taro-root, and a wood pigeon. Next they encounter what appears to be a wild-cat, though in fact it is a practically starving domestic one; shortly after this they discover a dilapidated hut, in which they find the skeleton of a man and a dog. There is an old pistol which they remove for their own use. After an exploration of a place called Diamond Cave, they kill a large sow and transfix the animal on a stick, lugging it back to their bower for a feast. Later the boys make a small boat and explore some of the minute adjacent islands.

Their next adventure is with two parties of raiding natives, one being pursued on to the island by the other. Thanks to the heroism of Jack, the boys rescue an important chief, Tararo, and a beautiful girl, Avatea. The natives depart happily, and shortly after this the boys see the sail of a schooner coming towards the island. On closer inspection this proves to be a pirate ship, and the boys take to the underwater cavern and hide. Ralph emerges, thinking the pirates have gone, and is immediately seized, brutally bound, and flung on board the pirates' boat.

The Captain, however, pretends that he is not a pirate but a sandal-wood trader; he is gradually impressed by Ralph's forthrightness and courage, and the boy becomes an active member of the crew, making friends with one of the better type of cut-throats, whose nickname is Bloody Bill. Ralph discovers how the Captain treats the natives, whether they have been converted to Christianity or not. He is a ruthless profiteer.

Eventually they come to an island, where the Captain negotiates with the chief, Romata, for wood-cutting rights, and here Ralph meets his old friend Tararo. He learns from him that Avatea, the Samoan girl the boys had earlier saved, has upset Tararo by falling in love with a native chief (later, we learn, converted to Christianity) whom Tararo hates. Shortly afterwards Ralph

overhears a conversation between the Captain and the mate in which it is apparent that the Captain intends to raid and betray the natives, sailing the schooner close to the shore and bringing his heavy gun to bear on them. Ralph tells Bill of the plan, and they arrange to thwart it.
They succeed. The Captain and many of the crew are captured and killed, and in the fight Bill is wounded. He and Ralph alone get back to the schooner, and Bill later dies of his wounds. Ralph, managing the schooner himself, gets back to the coral island and is reunited with Jack and Peterkin. Jack chivalrously wishes to find Avatea and see to it that she is made happy by marrying the man she loves. They make for the island, reach it, treat with the natives on behalf of Avatea with the help of a missionary, and are eventually taken by the natives and imprisoned. They wait for death but, to their surprise, are released by the tribe, who have just been converted to Christianity. All ends happily, and Avatea marries her young Christian chief.

From: *G. Handley,* Brodie's Notes on W. Golding's *Lord of the Flies,* Pan Books, London 1976, p. 1f.

**Annotations:**
*strapping* healthy looking – *mischievous* teasing, fun-loving, light-hearted – *to fend for o. s.* to look after o. s. – *shark* large, dangerous sea-fish – *dilapidated* falling to pieces – *to lug* to pull a heavy weight – *bower* (here:) shelter – *minute* [mai'nju:t]: very small, tiny – *adjacent* lying near or next to sth. – *to raid* to make a surprise attack – *to negotiate* to have discussions with sb. – *to thwart* to obstruct, frustrate (a plan) – *to treat with sb.* to discuss or arrange with sb. – *to release* to set free

*Student Paper No. 4:*
*Thomas Hobbes' Leviathan*

**Thomas Hobbes, The Leviathan**

The clearest model for Golding's thesis of the inevitability of the children's movement towards savagery is Thomas Hobbes' "The Leviathan" (1651). Hobbes (1588–1679) was an immensely influential political theorist. . . . In "The Leviathan" Hobbes asserted that man is intrinsically selfish. He denied that man is by nature a social being (as the Greek philosopher Aristotle had maintained) and upheld instead that each individual is fundamentally guided by self-interest. As Hobbes puts it, 'I put for a generall inclination of all mankind, a perpetuall and restlesse desire of Power after power, that ceaseth only in Death' (The Leviathan, Part 1, Chapter XI). To counter the anarchy which man's selfishness would create if there were no checks and balances to restrain it, we adopt, according to Hobbes, certain 'articles of peace' which impose restrictions on individual liberty. To see that these articles are implemented, an external power is entrusted with absolute authority, including the right to punish.

This power, in *Lord of the Flies,* is initially entrusted to Ralph by the common consent of the other children. When, however, he proves too ineffective as a leader he is displaced by the more ruthless figure of Jack. Hobbes suggests that the people's loyalty to the sovereign need only last as long as his authority effectively protects them. If his authority fails then they have the right to replace him by someone more competent. Hobbes denies that any man possesses an instinct to do good or to feel loyalty or to defend his friend. When these things occur it can only be as an act of self-interest. The leader, if he should fail the people in any way, cannot presume on the support or love of anyone. "... what argument of madness can there be greater than to clamour, strike and throw stones at our best friends?" The multitude, he says, "will clamour, fight against, and destroy those, by whom all their life-time before, they have been protected, and secured from injury. And if this be Madnesse in the multitude, it is the same in every particular man." (The Leviathan, Part I, Chapter VIII. p. 47)

Jack's lack of expertise in blowing the conch and his growing neglect of the symbolic authority with which it has been invested clearly point to his abuse of social custom. By the end of the novel Jack is well on his way to establishing a tyranny. He has been able – according to the Hobbesian notion that no sovereign can depend upon the loyalty of his people if he has ceased to protect them – to subvert the other children, to win them away from Ralph, and to establish a system of 'government' depending on the strict maintenance of his tyrannical 'justice'. He metes out summary justice to any opponent – Piggy dies, Ralph is hounded, Wilfred is beaten, Samneric possibly tortured. He wields his authority by pandering to the fear of his subjects and offering them outlets for their apprehension. Under his rule the children have festivals and rites of a kind which Ralph can see only as a distraction from what ought to be everyone's principal objective: rescue.

From: *Alastair Niven: William Golding, Lord of the Flies,* York Notes, Longman, 1980, p. 38f.

## Annotations/Vocabulary

*Chapter I*

**p. 7** *lagoon:* a salt water lake separated from the sea by sandbanks or reefs (as found in the South Pacific)

*school sweater, grey shirt:* part of the boys' school uniform, (The boys were probably travelling as a group of school children to be evacuated from a war.)

*to trail:* here: to let hang down

*to plaster:* to stick

*scar:* here: the long, wide line of smashed trees made by the crashing aircraft (Schneise)

*creepers:* Schlingpflanzen

*witch:* Hexe

*trunk:* stem of a tree

*caught up:* here: entangled, stuck fast

*to jerk:* to pull up

*the Home Counties:* the counties around London (Kent, Essex, Surrey, Middlesex)

*greasy:* here: dirty

*wind-breaker:* jacket to give protection from the wind

*plump:* rounded, fat

*megaphone:* portable amplifier (loudspeaker)

**p. 8** *startled:* here: alarmed

*pilot:* here: person who flies an aircraft

*passenger tube:* (detachable) part of a plane where the passengers are seated

*to peer at:* to look at

*casual:* nonchalant (lässig)

*offhand:* casual, curt

*jagged:* zersplittert

**p. 9** *it wasn't half dangerous (sl.):* it was very dangerous

*to trip over sth.:* to stumble

*asthma* ['æsmə]: chronic chest disease marked by difficult breathing and a cough

*specs (coll.):* spectacles, glasses

*them fruit:* (Piggy has eaten too much fruit and now has diarrhoea! His English is sub-standard; he is a Cockney and often makes grammatical mistakes e.g. p. 8, l. 8; p. 8, l. 32; p. 9, l. 21 etc.)

*to crouch:* to sit down, to squat

*tangled:* mixed up

*foliage:* all the leaves of plants, bushes, trees

**p. 10** *to disentangle:* to free from (the creepers)

*grunt:* rough sound, esp. of pigs

*fledged:* here: lined, fringed
*sapling:* young tree
*flinked:* (made up word) to send up a white spray
*bow-stave:* bent curve
*tummy (coll):* stomach

**p. 11** *pile:* heap (of sand)
*Piggy:* typical nickname for a fat boy

**p. 12** *platform:* flat surface at a higher level than the surrounding landscape
*jetty:* landing-place for a ship

**p. 13** *weed:* sea-weed, dt. Seetang
*whizzoh (sl.):* schoolboy expression of delight
*ledge:* narrow, horizontal shelf of cliff
*You can't half swim (sl.):* Du kannst aber toll schwimmen
*sucks to ... (sl.):* (expressing contempt) zum Kuckuck mit ..., ich pfeife auf ...

**p. 14** *humble:* demütig
*the Navy:* the officers and men of a country's warships
*(to get) leave:* time off from war duty
*to flush:* to blush, get red in the face

**p. 16** *a-bubble:* (made-up word) bubbling over with excitement
*conch* [kɔŋk, kɔntʃ]: the large spiral shell of a shellfish (Muschel)
*ever so v. (coll.):* extremely v.
*fulcrum* ['fulkrəm]: point on which a lever turns (Drehpunkt)

**p. 17** *jutting abdomen:* sticking out (protruding) belly

**p. 18** *to fart:* furzen
*diaphram* ['daiəfrəm]: Zwerchfell
*to squeal:* to give a shrill cry like a pig
*undergrowth:* shrubs and bushes growing among taller trees
*wubber:* a made-up word suggesting a sighing sound
*tusk:* long pointed (elephant's) tooth (wie Elfenbein)

**p. 19** *digit:* here: finger
*to conceal:* to hide
*to gorge:* to stuff into
*to frown:* die Stirn in Falten legen

**p. 20** *bat:* Fledermaus
*garments:* clothes

**p. 21** *hambone frill:* ornamental border on a dress (Rüschen)
*choir:* [kwaiə]: group of schoolchildren trained to sing together

**p. 22** *to throw a faint (sl.):* ohnmächtig werden
*Gib:* Gibraltar

*Addis:* Addis Ababa, capital of Ethiopia
*matins:* morning service in an Anglican church
*the precentor:* choir leader

**p.23** *chapter chorister:* cathedral choir-boy
*head boy:* here: choir prefect
*C-sharp:* das hohe C

**p.24** *mortification:* humiliation (Demütigung)

**p.25** *togs (sl.):* garments, clothes (Klamotten)

**p.27** *mirage* [mi'ra:ʒ]: optical illusion (Fata Morgana)
*icing on a cake:* Zuckerguß

**p.28** *askew:* not straight
skewed: twisted, turned to one side
*wacco, wizard, smashing:* schoolboy slang expressing enthusiasm

**p.29** *under-dusk:* Halbdunkel
*defiles:* narrow ways
*screes:* loose stones (Geröll)

**p.30** *golly (sl.):* exclamation of surprise
*cirque:* natural amphitheatre

**p.31** *astern* [ə'stə:n]: backward

**p.33** *sticking a pig:* to kill with a spear

**p.34** *daring them to c.:* challenging them, suggesting that they haven't the courage to do s.th.

*Chapter II*

**p.35** *smart:* pain
*to discard:* to throw off
*to clear one's throat:* sich räuspern

**p.36** *to convey:* here: to express
*to challenge:* herausfordern
*whee-oh, wacco, bong, doink:* schoolboys' sounds indicating punishment

**p.37** *a trumpet-thing:* the megaphone
*intent:* eager, earnest
*to slant in:* to fall in sideways

**p.38** *Treasure Island:* Robert Louis Stevenson's classic adventure book (1883) about pirates on a tropical island
*Swallows and Amazons:* an outdoor adventure story by Arthur Ransome (1930) describing English children discovering an island in the Lake

District. Ransome wrote a whole series (1930-1947) of similar adventure books.
*The Coral Island:* a well-known adventure book by R. M. Ballantyne about English schoolboys wrecked on a tropical island (1858)
*a shrimp of a boy:* a very small boy, a little dot

**p. 39** *to induce:* to persuade
*grave:* serious

**p. 40** *dubiety:* doubts
*nightmare:* bad dream, dt. Alptraum
*exasperation:* irritation, anger
*annoyed:* angry, irritated
*to compel:* to force

**p. 41** *navy:* a country's warships
*the Navy:* the military forces organized for fighting on sea
*to smirk:* to give a silly smile
*borne on:* carried by

**p. 42** *to sway:* to move, to swing
*scornful:* showing contempt
*to caress:* to stroke affectionately
*swathes* [sweiðz]: here: rows of felled trees

**p. 43** *soil:* earth
*to decay:* to go bad (verrotten)
*cap of maintenance:* here: head covering worn by the choir boys as part of their choir uniform
*beret* ['berei]: military head-dress (Baskenmütze)
*to inch:* to move by inches, i.e. bit by bit
*limb:* here: branch
*burden:* load, heavy weight
*content:* satisfaction
*to dump:* to drop

**p. 44** *to spin:* to turn quickly
*mime:* imitation
*shriek:* shrill scream

**p. 45** *officious:* eager to help
*to grope:* to feel about as one does in the dark
*blur:* indistinct spots
*the immediate end:* the nearest goal, their only purpose
*fruit claimed them:* i.e. they had diarrhoea from eating too much fruit, and had to crouch down in the bushes!
*savage:* fierce, cruel, wild
*damp:* moist, a little wet

**p.46** *panting:* breathing quickly
*coign:* [kɔin]: place from which one has a good view
*a fat lot (sl.):* a great deal, very much
*shut up (vulg.):* hold your tongue (halt's Maul)
*taut* [tɔ:t]: tightly stretched

**p.47** *to assent:* to agree
*sooty:* schwarz vom Ruß
*alto:* male singing voice between tenor and treble; countertenor
*treble:* boy's voice with the highest part in a piece of music
*gloomy:* düster

**p.48** *recrimination:* counter accusation
*to festoon:* umranken
*bole:* trunk of a tree
*squirrel:* small, bushy-tailed, tree-climbing animal
*to gnaw:* to bite at

**p.49** *to caper:* to jump about playfully
*awe:* fearful respect
*bleak:* cheerless
*pall* [pɔ:l]: heavy cloth spread over a coffin; hence: a pall of smoke = a thick cloud of smoke

**p.50** *it wasn't half cold (sl.):* it was very cold
*to growl:* to make a low, threatening sound

**p.51** *to pinch (sl.):* to take without permission, to steal
*agonized:* here: erstarrten

*Chapter III*

**p.52** *tendril:* Ranke
*node:* point on tree stem where a leaf grows out
*nostrils:* openings into the nose

**p.53** *gaudy:* brightly coloured
*abyss:* Abgrund
*furtive:* secretive
*avid:* greedy, eager
*pallor:* paleness (of face)
*droppings:* animal excrements
*vicissitude:* change (from success to failure)
*to swear:* to curse, to use obscene words

**p.54** *contraption:* strange-looking device
*shelter:* here: hut
*contrite:* schuldbewußt

**p. 55** *the littluns:* contraction of 'the little ones'
*tell 'em off:* tell them off (schimpf mit ihnen)
*compulsion:* innerer Zwang

**p. 56** *antagonism:* opposition, animosity
*dashed (sl.):* damned

**p. 57** *batty, crackers (sl.):* mad, crazy
*incredulous:* unbelieving

**p. 58** *declivity:* downward slope
*bewildered:* puzzled, confused
*rapt:* carried away

**p. 59** *to buzz off (sl.):* to walk off, to go away
*to get fed up (sl.):* to have enough and become bored (die Nase voll haben)
*queer:* strange

**p. 60** *tacit:* unspoken
*tacit consent:* stillschweigendes Einverständnis
*baffled:* confused, mixed up, puzzled
*tread:* way of walking, steps

**p. 61** *pasture:* grassland for cattle
*to lug:* to pull
*inscrutable:* sth. that cannot be understood
*to founder:* to sink

**p. 62** *susurration:* whispering
*riotous:* here: wild
*sepals:* outer leaves of a flower bud
*scent:* smell of flowers

*Chapter IV*

**p. 63** *momentum:* here: power
*stunted:* bent

**p. 64** *biguns:* contraction of 'big ones'
*diarrhoea* [ˌdaiə'riə]: Durchfall
*summons:* order to appear
*corporate:* united in a group

**p. 65** *belligerence* [be'lidʒərəns]: tendency to fight
*chastisement:* punishment
*unease:* bad conscience

**p. 66** *Pacific tide:* the regular rise and fall in the level of the Pacific ocean (a geographic hint that the island is somewhere in the South Seas)
*to quest:* to try to find

*incursion:* invasion
*to strew:* to scatter
*detritus:* sand or gravel produced by wearing away from rocks etc.
*to scavenge:* to search among refuse material
*vagrant:* wandering
*the hams:* (coll.): the behind, buttocks

**p. 67** *to croon:* to hum or sing gently
*fronds:* palm leaves
*token:* symbol
*preposterous:* contrary to reason or sense
*setter:* long-haired dog trained to stand motionless for hunting

**p. 68** *mere:* pond
*clay:* Lehm
*charcoal:* Holzkohle
*dazzle paint:* Tarnfarbe
*moth:* winged insect attracted by light

**p. 69** *Samneric:* The names 'Sam and Eric' blended together, indicating that the identical twins operate almost as one person
*to appal:* to fill with fear and terror
*to snarl:* to show the teeth and growl (usu. of dogs)
*to compel s.o.:* to force s.o. to do sth., here: to hold in fascination

**p. 70** *shock-headed:* having rough, untidy hair
*baldness:* being without hair
*to pull s.o.'s leg (coll.):* to make fun of s.o.

**p. 71** *belly-flop (coll.):* unsuccessful dive into the water (Bauchlandung)
*to irk:* to annoy
*footling:* insignificant, trifling
*balm:* ointment for soothing pain (Balsam)
*clumsy:* ungraceful and not skilful
*to make a bolt for:* to dash forward
*to swerve:* to change direction suddenly
*to clench:* to close tightly

**p. 72** *funnel:* ship's chimney
*ravenous:* greedy
*to slew:* to turn round
*shallow:* not deep

**p. 73** *to rasp:* to scratch

**p. 74** *the bloody fire (sl.):* 'bloody' is often used as a bad swearword in English
*audible:* loud enough to be heard
*stake:* long, pointed piece of wood
*to gut:* to take the intestines out

**p.75** *to snivel:* to cry in a miserable, whining way
*a nick in the hilt:* a notch in the handle of the knife (counting the number of his killings!)

**p.76** *charitable:* here: generous
*to buzz:* to make a sound (of talking)

**p.77** *exhilaration:* high spirits, enthusiasm
*bolting:* here: aggressive
*vicious:* spiteful, with evil intent
*humiliation:* putting to shame (Demütigung)

**p.78** *to smack:* to strike (with open hand)
*gyration:* moving round in circles

**p.79** *verbal trick:* (Jack's apology!)
*to assert:* here: to maintain

**p.80** *to skewer:* to fasten or stick on
*to dribble:* to have one's mouth water
*odd:* here: occasional
*wet (sl.):* weak
*ha'porth:* a halfpenny-worth, i.e. practically nothing

**p.81** *nob (sl.):* head
*a fourpenny one (sl.):* a heavy blow

*Chapter V*

**p.83** *wearisomeness:* tiredness, dullness
*to jeer:* to mock, laugh rudely at
*maze:* labyrinth
*urgency:* need for haste

**p.84** *convulsion of the mind:* here: violent feeling of disgust
*perpetual:* never ending
*triangle* ['traiæŋgl]: geometrical figure with three straight sides
*twister:* here: a twisted (bent, curved) tree stem
*apex* ['eipeks]: top or highest point (e.g. of a triangle)

**p.85** *ludicrous:* ridiculous
*brains:* intellect
*to bleach:* to make white
*solemnity:* seriousness

**p.86** *to put things straight:* to make things clear (and put them right)

**p.87** *tottery:* unsteady
*to be taken short:* to have to go to the toilet suddenly

**p.89** *row* [rau]: here: tumult
*you can jolly well go (coll.):* you may as well go
*bogie:* evil spirit

**p.90** *cry-babies and sissies (sl.):* cowards

**p.91** *in a sec (sl.):* in a second, immediately afterwards

**p.92** *sympathy:* compassion

**p.93** *derisive:* showing mockery

**p.94** *condemnation:* negative criticism, ridicule
*Percival Wemys Madison, etc.:* the little boy is rattling off his name and address as his parents may have told him to if he got lost

**p.95** *to pucker:* to wrinkle up
*my foot (sl.):* exclamation like 'rubbish', 'nonsense'

**p.96** *sough* [sʌf]: whispering sound

**p.97** *perilous:* dangerous
*nuts (sl.):* exclamation meaning 'nonsense'
*the one crude syllable:* "shit"

**p.98** *gimme:* give me
*talking out of turn:* talking before one is permitted time to speak

**p.99** *fat slug (sl.):* a very offensive description; Piggy is compared to a fat, slow moving snail

**p.100** *bollocks (sl.):* a contemptuous expression meaning: nonsense (ich pfeife auf die Regeln)
*mock hunting:* imitation hunting

**p.101** *three blind mice:* Ralph is expressing the helplessness of the three boys by quoting the words of the nursery rhyme "Three blind mice, see how they run . . ."

**p.102** *dunno:* don't know
*you got him over the fire:* your point with regard to the fire was convincing
*wail:* shrill crying
*gibbering:* fast, meaningless talking

*Chapter VI*

**p.104** *save:* except
*parachute* ['pærəʃu:t]: a device made of cloth, used for a jump from an aircraft
*to dangle:* to hang or swing loosely
*limbs* [limz]: arms and legs

**p.105** *tinder wood:* dry wood that easily catches fire from a spark

**p.106** *waxy (sl.):* angry

**p.107** *idly:* here: without intention
*fabric:* textile material, woven cloth

**p.108** *to squawk (of birds):* to utter a loud, harsh cry as when hurt or frightened

**p.109** *furry:* covered with fur (animal's hair)

**p.110** *sucks to . . . (sl.):* meaning: 'what do the littluns matter?'

**p.111** *like what's its name:* Ralph is thinking either of an ape, like a gorilla, or of characters made popular by film series, such as Tarzan (the man who lived with apes) or King Kong (the giant ape who was taken from some Pacific island to be exhibited in America, and who caused all sorts of sensations)
*embroiled:* mixed up in a quarrel

**p.112** *exasperation:* irritation

**p.113** *incredulity:* disbelief
*diffident:* shy, not having much self-confidence
*to slacken one's pace:* to walk more slowly
*to snigger:* to laugh cynically

**p.115** *leviathan* [li'vaiəθən]: in the Bible: a monstrous sea animal of enormous size; here: the powerful tide

**p.116** *plinth:* a square base or block on which a column stands
*guano:* excrement of sea birds
*to grate:* to make a harsh noise

**p.117** *you're nuts (sl.):* you're crazy
*bruised:* injured by a blow

**p.119** *off your rockers (sl.):* crazy, out of your senses, mad
*mutinous:* rebellious

*Chapter VII*

**p.120** *dun:* dull, greyish brown
*covert:* thick undergrowth (in which animals hide)

**p.121** *scurfy with brine:* covered with white salt from the sea

**p.122** *to numb* [nʌm]: to deaden
*obtuseness:* here: insensitivity

**p.123** *to bunch:* to form a group, to keep together
*to loiter:* to walk slowly
*Chatham, Devonport:* important naval bases in the south of England
*the moors:* wild, uncultivated, usually hilly and heather-covered countryside

**p. 124** *to skip:* to leave out
*to scrabble:* here: to crawl
*to nudge:* to push
*to intimidate:* to cause fear, to scare
*boar:* male pig
*apprehension:* understanding, here: fear of things to come

**p. 125** *to wallop (sl.):* to hit hard
*Berengaria:* wife of Richard I; she is said to have sucked her husband's battle wounds († 1230)

**p. 126** *mock rush:* a pretended rush
*to brandish:* to wave about
*bum (sl.):* bottom, buttocks
*rugger (coll.):* rugby

**p. 127** *funk (sl.):* coward

**p. 128** *to scale:* here: to climb up

**p. 130** *to bring up the rear:* to be last

**p. 131** *curse:* Fluch

**p. 133** *windy (sl.):* scared, frightened
*to rock:* to swing backwards and forwards
*impervious:* unmoved
*fuming:* in a state of anger

**p. 134** *to bulge:* here: to move and swell

**p. 135** *nausea* ['nɔ:siə]: feeling of sickness
*paralysed:* unable to move

**p. 136** *leaden* ['ledn]: heavy (like lead) (bleiern)
*ape:* tailless monkey, e.g. a gorilla

*Chapter VIII*

**p. 139** *tremor:* thrill and trembling

**p. 140** *Ralph's lot:* the group of boys around Ralph

**p. 142** *no go (sl.):* hopeless situation

**p. 143** *stub:* short remaining end
*to scurry:* to hurry, to run with short, quick steps
*sodden:* moist and sticky

**p. 145** *to the quick:* to the sensitive flesh below the nails
*embers:* small pieces of burning wood in a dying fire
*jolt:* sudden jerk, shock

**p.146** *cracked (sl.):* mad

**p.147** *fervour:* earnestness
*bloated:* swollen
*sensuous:* with all their senses

**p.148** *bliss:* perfect happiness
*bladder:* here: bag
*to burrow:* here: to move and push their heads (to find the sow's teats)
*drove:* group of animals
*demented:* mad (with fear)

**p.149** *torment:* torture, pain
*to hurl:* to throw violently
*to prod:* to push or poke
*to subside:* to go down, sink, become quiet
*he flinked his hands:* (made up word) he moved his hand and showed his palms
*to reek:* to smell strongly
*the stuff:* here: the blood!

**p.150** *to paunch:* die Eingeweide ausnehmen
*to sneak up:* to get close as quietly as possible (sich heranschleichen)

**p.151** *to skewer:* here: to put on a stake
*to conceal:* to hide

**p.152** *to gorge:* to eat greedily
*to alight:* here: to land
*"Lord of the Flies":* (the pig's head), a translation of Hebrew 'Beelzebub', the devil
*temple:* Schläfe

**p.153** *vexed:* annoyed, distressed

**p.155** *crimson:* deep red
*savages:* members of a primitive tribe

**p.156** *ass-mar:* naughty mispronunciation of 'asthma'
*to raid:* to make a surprise attack

**p.158** *fancy thinking ...:* imagine one could think
*his eyes could not break away:* he could not take his eyes off
*to wobble:* to move from side to side
*one of his times was coming on:* one of Simon's fits of fainting (cf. p. 22, l. 2 and l. 8f.)

**p.159** *we shall do you:* we shall kill you

**p. 160** *brassy:* messingfarben
*to drain:* to flow away from
*to brood:* here: to hang heavily
*to prosper:* to do well, to be successful

**p. 161** *interspersed with:* dotted with
*glum:* gloomy, sad
*buffet:* gust, blow
*to cuff:* to hit

**p. 162** *looming:* threatening
*to squirt:* to blow or spit water out of one's mouth
*meek:* patient, unprotesting

**p. 163** *keep your hair on (sl.):* keep calm
*to protrude:* to stick out

**p. 164** *idol* ['aidl]: image (usu. in wood or stone) of a god; also: false god
*bourdon:* regular noise of the water breaking over the distant reef
*chunk:* thick piece
*derision:* mockery

**p. 165** *succulent:* juicy, tasting good
*to sizzle:* to make a hissing sound when roasting
*spit:* roasting spear
*to stoop:* to bend down
*to saunter:* to walk unhurriedly

**p. 167** *to flinch:* to move back
*to charge:* here: to attack
*club:* here: Knüppel
*to hem in:* to confine, enclose, surround

**p. 168** *unendurable:* more than one can bear
*abominable:* horrible

**p. 169** *to surge after:* to move after (like waves)
*ungainly:* clumsy, awkward
*to furrow:* to make lines in
*cleft:* crack (in a rock or the ground)
*minutely* [mai'nju:tli]: here: very slowly
*the shallows:* the part of the sea that is not deep
*to seep:* to trickle

**p. 171** *scab:* crust over a wound

**p. 173** *stricken:* overcome by grief
*loathing:* disgust

**p. 174** *to let on (sl.):* to reveal a secret; to tell

**p. 175** *to be challenged:* to be stopped and asked to explain who one is
*"Halt! Who goes there?":* the traditional challenge of sentries on watch

**p. 176** *lever:* Hebel
*sombre:* gloomy

**p. 177** *to disguise:* to change the appearance (to hide the identity)

**p. 179** *to beckon:* to call s.o.'s attention to sth.
*hearth (fig.):* fireside as representing security
*billow (fig.):* wave, here: cloud
*the reds:* the communists, probably the enemies in the war

**p. 180** *to cram:* here: to eat a lot
*to whisk:* to move quickly

**p. 181** *battered:* beaten out of shape
*to burrow:* here: to cover o.s.
*an oblong:* ein Rechteck
*spangles:* tiny shining specks (= the stars)
*Wiltshire* ['wiltʃə], *Devon:* counties in the south of England

**p. 182** *to skate:* to move (to another subject)
*barmy, round the bend, bomb happy, crackers (sl.):* mad, crazy

**p. 183** *to rebuke s.o.:* to tell s.o. off (jdn. tadeln)
*woebegone:* dismal looking
*to prowl:* to go about cautiously (in search of prey)

**p. 184** *piston:* Kolben
*to writhe:* to twist in pain
*to pound:* to strike, to hammer
*quavering:* trembling (voice)

**p. 185** *to bust:* to hit
*to holler:* to yell

**p. 186** *bowstave:* here: bent curve
*to turn cartwheels:* to turn somersaults sideways (radschlagen)
*to exult in sth.:* to enjoy a triumph

*Chapter XI*

**p. 187** *luminous:* bright
*myopia:* short-sightedness

**p. 189** *to be a sport:* to be fair, to show good sportsmanship

**p. 190** *to devastate:* to ruin

**p. 191** *propitiating:* besänftigend

**p. 192** *to limp:* to walk lamely or unevenly
*to scour:* to clean

**p. 193** *to dispose o.s.:* to place o.s. in suitable position

**p. 196** *lethal* ['li:θl]: death-bringing
*truculent* ['trʌkjulənt]: aggressive, looking for a fight
*pinnacles:* the highest parts of the castle rock
*to play the game:* to obey the rules

**p. 197** *cessation:* stopping

**p. 198** *his fringe:* Ralph's hair hanging over his eyes
*to bounce:* to jump (like a ball)
*ferocity:* savage cruelty

**p. 199** *menace:* threat
*to bristle with:* to exist in large numbers

**p. 200** *abandonment:* complete surrender to impulses
*to bound:* to jump, to bounce

**p. 201** *to wield:* to have and use

*Chapter XII*

**p. 202** *tapped:* verknotet
*to retrieve:* to find again, to get back

**p. 203** *to toss:* to throw
*pebble:* small stone

**p. 204** *inquisitive:* curious
*prickles of sensation:* Schauder
*to bob:* move up and down
*to lash:* to strike violently
*to wrench:* to twist and pull

**p. 205** *to ambush:* to attack
*to have pax (sl.):* peace, a momentary interruption of a game
*outcast:* homeless and friendless person, driven out from society

*to savour:* here: to enjoy
*to quiver:* to tremble

**p. 206** *eclipsed:* hidden
*shaft of a pit:* Kohlenschacht
*inimical:* unfriendly
*to hamper:* to hinder
*flurry:* sudden rush, nervous hurry

**p. 207** *to haul up:* to heave up
*to shove off (sl.):* to go away

**p. 208** *to push off (sl.):* to go away
*they will do you (sl.):* they will kill you
*dunno:* don't know

**p. 209** *to goad (fig.):* to drive on

**p. 210** *crutch:* Krücke
*to reel:* to walk unsteadily
*to tense:* to stiffen

**p. 211** *lair:* animal's resting place
*to ensconce o.s.:* to establish o.s. in a safe place
*to diddle:* to deceive
*mould:* here: dead leaves
*ululation:* loud howling
*brake:* here: thicket

**p. 212** *hushed:* subdued, quiet

**p. 213** *to trundle:* to roll
*diaphragm* ['daiəfræm]: Zwerchfell

**p. 214** *to moan:* to groan

**p. 215** *crepitation:* series of sharp, crackling sounds
*to double up:* to bend the body in pain

**p. 216** *to be baulked* [bɔ:kt]: to be held up (by an obstacle)

**p. 217** *simpleton:* fool
*excrutiating:* painful
*fathom:* (a measure:) six feet

**p. 218** *to thump:* to beat heavily
*to volley:* to shoot at the same time

**p. 220** *to ward off:* to keep away, avoid

**p. 221** *wary:* cautious
*cutter:* ship's boat, for use between ship and shore
*bow* [bau]: front end of a ship

*to haul up:* to pull up (the beach)
*rating:* here: sailor
*stern:* rear end of a ship
*to falter:* to waver, become irregular
*to squirm:* to twist and wriggle from embarrassment
*scarecrow:* Vogelscheuche
*ointment:* medicinal paste (Salbe)

**p. 223** *fleeting:* passing quickly
*trim:* neat and tidy (schmuck)
*cruiser* ['kru:zə]: fast warship

# Selected Bibliography


*Howard S. Babb:* The Novels of William Golding, Columbus, Ohio State Univ. Press, 1973

*James R. Baker:* William Golding: A Critical Study, N.Y., St. Martin's, 1965

*J. R. Baker / A. P. Ziegler (eds.):* William Golding's "Lord of the Flies", Casebook, N. Y., Putnam's, 1964

*John Beston:* A Comprehensive Outline of W. Golding's "LoF", N.Y., Harvard Outline Co., 1963

*Jack I. Biles:* Talk: Conversations with William Golding, N.Y., Harcourt Brace Jovanovich, 1970

*J. I. Biles / R. O. Evans (eds.):* William Golding. Some Critical Considerations. Univ. Press of Kentucky, 1978 (Detailed bibliography: pp. 238–283)

*Denis M. Calandra:* "Lord of the Flies", Notes, Lincoln, Nebraska, Cliff's Notes, 1971

*Arno Esch:* William Golding, Lord of the Flies, in: Der Englische Roman, Interpretationen, ed. Horst Oppel, Berlin, E. Schmidt Verlag, 1965

*A. D. Fleck:* The Golding Bough ..., in: On the Novel, ed. B. S. Benedikz, London, Dent, 1971

*Peter Freese:* Verweisende Zeichen in W. Goldings Lord of the Flies, DN Spr LXXI, 1972, S. 160–172

*N. Friedmann:* Form and Meaning in Fiction, Univ. of Georgia Press, 1975

*Liesel Hermes:* Literarische Lernziele im Englischunterricht der Sekundarstufe II am Beispiel der Romanbehandlung im Leistungskurs, in: Der Fremdsprachliche Unterricht, Heft 36, 4/1975, Klett, Stuttgart

*Liesel Hermes:* Der Roman im Englischunterricht, in: P. Freese/L. Hermes, Der Roman im Englischunterricht der Sekundarstufe II, Schöningh, Paderborn $^{2}$1981

*Leighton Hodson:* William Golding, Writers and Critics, No. 61, Edinburgh, Oliver and Boyd, 1969; N.Y., Capricorn, 1971

*Samuel Hynes:* William Golding, Columbia Univ. Press, 1964

*Frederick Jackson:* An Outline of "Lord of the Flies", Toronto, Forum House, 1968

*Frederick Jackson:* William Golding, Lord of the Flies, London, Coles Notes, 1970$^{2}$

*Arnold Johnston:* Of Earth and Darkness, The Novels of William Golding, Univ. of Missouri Press, Columbia, 1980

*Frank Kermode:* William Golding, in: On Contemporary Literature, ed. R. Kostelanetz, N.Y., Avon Books, 1964

*M. Kinkead-Weekes/I. Gregor:* William Golding, a critical study, London, Faber & Faber, 1974

*M. Lefkowitz, L. Eron, u. a.:* Growing Up to be Violent: A Study of the Development of Aggression, N.Y., Pergamon Press, 1977

*Stephen Medcalf:* William Golding, Writers and Their Work, No. 243, London, Longman, 1975

*William Nelson (ed.):* William Golding's "Lord of the Flies", A Source Book, N.Y., Odyssey, 1963
*Alastair Niven:* William Golding, Lord of the Flies, York Notes, Longman, 1980
*B. S. Oldsey / S. Weintraub:* The Art of William Golding, N.Y., Harcourt's, 1965
*Arno Plack:* Die Gesellschaft und das Böse, München, List, 1967
*Virginia Tiger:* William Golding, Lord of the Flies, in: The Dark Fields of Discovery, London, Calder & Boyars, 1974
*Hermann J. Weiand:* William Golding, Lord of the Flies, in: Insight V, Hirschgraben, 1981